module 4

H/IGCSE

Geography

Cambridge International Examinations

George Woodward, Principal Examiner for IGCSE and HIGCSE and **John Pallister**, A-level Geography examiner

Edited by **Di Barton**

CAMBRIDGE
UNIVERSITY PRESS

PUBLISHED BY THE PRESS SYNDICATE OF THE UNIVERSITY OF CAMBRIDGE
The Pitt Building, Trumpington Street, Cambridge, United Kingdom

CAMBRIDGE UNIVERSITY PRESS
The Edinburgh Building, Cambridge CB2 2RU, United Kingdom
40 West 20th Street, New York, NY 10011–4211, USA
10 Stamford Road, Oakleigh, VIC 3166, Australia
Ruiz de Alarcón 13, 28014 Madrid, Spain
Dock House, The Waterfront, Cape Town 8001, South Africa

http://www.cambridge.org

First published 2000, reprinted 2001, 2002

Printed in Cape Town, South Africa by Creda Communications

Typeface New Century Schoolbook 11.5/14 pt

A catalogue record for this book is available from the British Library

ISBN 0 521 78709 2 paperback

Acknowledgements

All line illustrations are by Anne Westoby, except the following: pages 8, 13b, 16, 26, 27, 28, 29, 30t, 30m, 30b, 32, 33, 34, 35, 36t, 36b, 39, 40, 43, 45, 46b, 51, 52, 53t, 53b, 93, 94, 95, courtesy of UCLES (redrawn by Anne Westoby); the diagram on page 30m is with permission from Morey D. *'Climate and Environmental Systems'* Union Hyman Ltd.; the diagrams on pages 75 and 82 are after Bowen, A. and Pallister, J., *'Tackling Geography Coursework'*, Hodder; the diagram on page 90 is based on Tucker, M. *'The Field Classification of Sedimentary Rocks'*, Open University Press, 1982.

The map references on page 2 and subsequent pages refer to the Shamva (Zimbabwe) 1:50 000 map, published by the Surveyor-General, Zimbabwe, 1989.

Photographs are as follows: pages 17, 68, 80, courtesy of Ray Howarth; pages 74, 79, courtesy of John Pallister.

We acknowledge the assistance of Ray Howarth in the revision of Unit 3.

The assignment described on pages 87 to 91 is courtesy of UCLES.

Every effort has been made to contact the owners of the copyright of all the information contained in this book, but, if for any reason, any acknowledgements have been omitted, the publishers ask those concerned to contact them.

Contents

Introduction

Welcome to Module 4 of IGCSE / HIGCSE Geography. This is the final module of the series which will help you to prepare for both the International General Certificate of Secondary Education (IGCSE) and the Higher International General Certificate of Secondary Education (HIGCSE) in Geography. Before starting this module, you should have completed Modules 1, 2 and 3. The diagram below shows how this module fits into the IGCSE / HIGCSE Geography course as a whole.

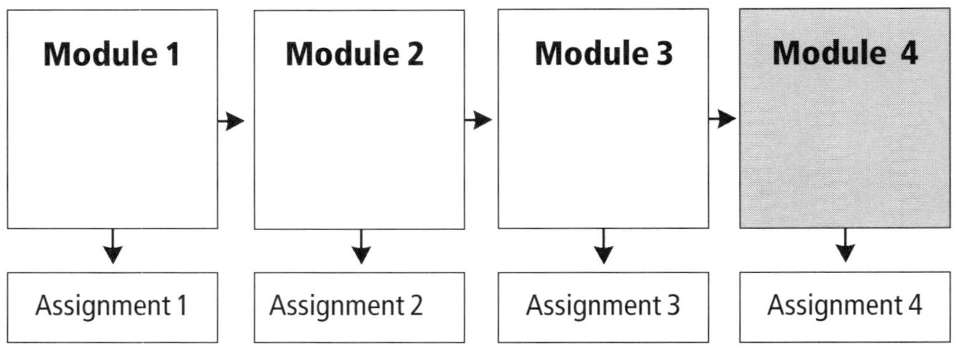

In the first unit of this module we will look at topographical maps to learn how to read and extract information from them which will help you to understand physical and human landscapes.

In Unit 2 we will be seeing different ways of representing data and learning how to extract information from these in order to further your understanding of the subject.

In Unit 3 we will discuss enquiry skills. Here you will see how to choose and organise coursework assignments. The techniques involved in collecting and interpreting data, as well as its presentation, will be outlined.

Unit 4 looks at the skills which will be tested in the examinations and also suggests some ways to help you to successfully read and understand what is required by different types of examination questions. It also includes advice about examination papers in general.

The introduction to Module 1 explained how the four modules relate to each other to present you with an all-round approach to the study of IGCSE and HIGCSE Geography. It is useful to repeat this information and to emphasise the key role played by the content of Module 4. The diagram below shows how this module relates to the others.

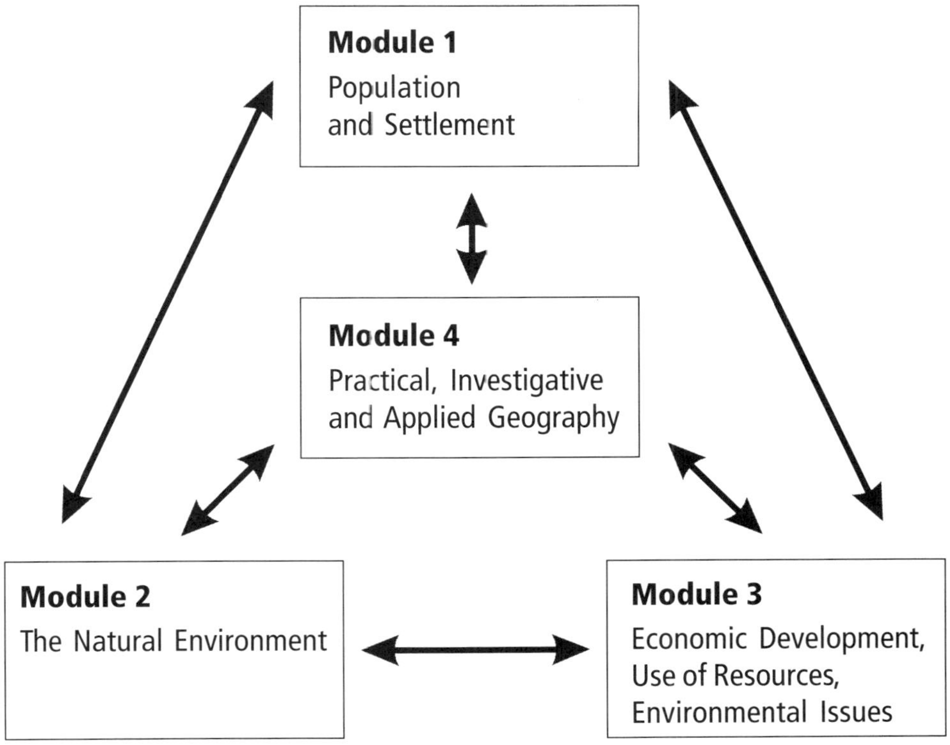

You can see from this diagram that all parts of geography are related and you will gain most from your studies when you keep this in mind.

The content of Module 4 plays a direct role in preparing you for questions on practical skills in Papers 3 and 5 in IGCSE, as well as Question 7 (map reading and interpretation) on Paper 2 and Paper 4 in HIGCSE. In addition, these practical skills should be coupled with the content of Unit 3 of this module to prepare you for geographical enquiries pursued in coursework assignments in Paper 4 of IGCSE and Paper 3 of HIGCSE.

Module 4 also has another important part to play, in helping you with your preparation for the other papers in both examinations. All through Modules 1 – 3 reference is made to geographical information given in a variety of forms – maps, diagrams, graphs, tables of data, written material, photographs and other pictorial presentations. You need to know how to read and interpret all of these. You must therefore continually refer to the details contained within Module 4 as you work your way through the other three modules. It is only by making continual cross-references from one module to another that you can fully prepare for the examinations.

Some of the equipment you will need when you use this module is listed below:

- A notebook and pen to make notes as you work your way through the units and to answer questions set in the activities.
- A pencil and rubber are useful if you want to write information on graphs, diagrams, etc. that are printed in this module, as part of the activities.

- A ruler, set square and protractor are essential. As well as being necessary in attempting some of the questions set in the activities, this equipment, along with the pencil and rubber, are needed in the examination room when you attempt Paper 3 in IGCSE and Paper 4 (The Alternative to Coursework) in HIGCSE.
- Equipment for fieldwork enquiries as part of coursework, described in Unit 3.
- A dictionary is useful to look up new words. This module, like the other three, contains glossary definitions of unfamiliar words used in the text. A dictionary would, however, help you to understand any other words that may be new to you.
- An atlas is also recommended to look up places. Remember that you are not allowed to take an atlas into the examination room.

Use the table below to help you to keep a record of your progress through Module 4. Each unit is followed by a Check your progress exercise. These should be completed and your answers compared with the information given in the Answers section at the end of this module. Remember that you need to plan time to study each unit and complete the end-of-module assignment.

Finally it is worth stressing again that the content of this module will directly help you to prepare for papers in both IGCSE and HIGCSE. This module will also give you a clearer understanding of the topics discussed in the other three modules. When you have finished the whole course, you will need to go back and revise each module, including this one, before writing the exam. Make sure that you have a regular study plan for the next few months, and try to have regular study periods during each week. Good luck!

HIGCSE/IGCSE Geography Module 4

Unit no.	Unit title	Unit studied	Check your progress completed	Assignment completed	Revised for exam
1	Topographical maps and their interpretation				
2	The representation and interpretation of data				
3	Enquiry skills				
4	Preparing for the examination				

Unit 1

Topographical maps and their interpretation

We all enjoy looking at maps, whether it is to find out the attractions of an area when on holiday, or when walking, cycling or motoring. We all have in our minds a number of different maps; our route from home to school, to the local shops or the sports stadium and where other places lie in relation to each other. Being aware of these relationships is an important part of our daily life.

Maps are exciting to look at and we can always find something on a map which attracts our interest. A topographical map shows aspects of the physical landscape including relief, drainage and features of natural vegetation. In addition it reveals evidence of human occupation of an area with details of settlement, agricultural and other uses of the land. This information enables us to have a better understanding of areas.

To make the most of your study of maps, you need to learn some basic skills. When you have acquired these, you can then proceed to see patterns and relationships between the various features shown on maps.

So that you can work through this unit, make sure you have a copy of the map that accompanies this book. The map is of Shamva, Zimbabwe.

This unit is divided into the following sections:

A	Reading symbols
B	Locating features
C	Giving directions
D	Measuring distances
E	Determining heights
F	Calculating gradients
G	Interpreting cross-sections
H	Interpreting physical and human landscapes

In this unit you will learn to use a topographical map to:

- read the symbols given in the key
- locate features
- describe directions between locations
- measure distances
- determine heights
- calculate gradients
- interpret and label cross-sections
- interpret the main features of the physical landscape
- relate the physical background to human responses
- interpret the nature of the human landscape.

A Reading symbols

Hint
All large-scale maps chosen in the examinations will always contain a full key.

Symbols are signs used on topographical maps to represent features on the ground. Sometimes abbreviations are used instead of symbols. Examples of the use of abbreviations are given in the key to the Shamva map such as PS representing a Police Station and PO a Post Office.

B Locating features

In order to locate features on a topographical map, reference needs to be made to grid lines. These are the numbered lines crossing a map from west to east and from south to north.

- Vertical grid lines are known as **eastings** – so called because they are numbered from west to east.
- Horizontal grid lines are known as **northings** – these are numbered from south to north.
- Used together, grid lines define a series of grid squares on a map.
- A grid reference gives the location or position of a feature on a map.
- In all grid references the eastings are given before the northings.

Hint
You should be able to give both a 4 figure and a 6 figure grid reference.

Hint
The Shamva map is folded and inserted separately in this book.

To identify the grid square containing Nyagui School in the south east of the Shamva map:

- Give the number of the easting and then the number of the northing which intersect at its south west corner.
- The **4-figure grid reference** for this grid square is 5671.

For a precise location of Nyagui School in this grid square, we need to give a **6-figure grid reference**.

- First of all identify the grid square by a 4-figure grid reference, explained above.
- This grid square is bounded by eastings 56 and 57. This space needs to be divided into 10 equal parts. The divisions between these 10 spaces are numbered 1 – 9. The easting for Nyagui School is 565.
- The grid square is also bounded by northings 71 and 72. The space between northings 71 and 72 is also divided into 10 equal parts. Again the divisions between the spaces are numbered 1 – 9. The northing for Nyagui School is 715.

  The 6-figure reference for Nyagui School is 565715.

Hint
In all grid references give the easting before the northing.

ACTIVITY 1

This is your first activity. Write down your answers to all activities in a notebook. This will give you practice in writing out answers as you will have to do in the examination. The answers are on page 23. Check your answers when you have completed all of the questions.

Refer to the Shamva map and answer the following:

1 What is the name of the hill located in grid square 4884?

2 Name the estate located in grid square 4184.

3 State the named building found at grid reference 473874.

4 Give the value of the spot height at grid reference 539857.

5 What is the symbol located at grid reference 457782?

C Giving directions

Direction on topographical maps may be given as follows:

- by using compass points to give **compass directions**. Here reference is made to the main compass points of north, south, west and east. Other points in between give directions in more detail and include north east, south east, south west and north west. Even more precision can be given if reference is made to points in between these, such as north north east. See Figure 1.1 below.

Hint
You will complete Figures 1.1 and 1.2 in Activity 2.

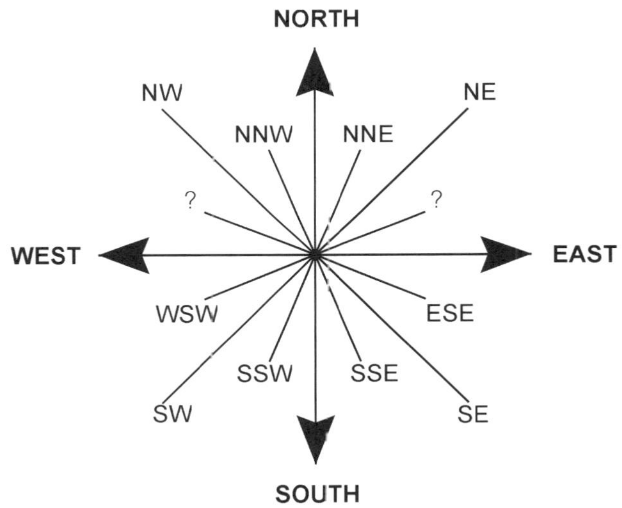

Figure 1.1 The sixteen compass points

- by using bearings from grid north. These bearings are known as **grid bearings**. They are given in degrees working clockwise from 0° or grid north. See Figure 1.2 below.

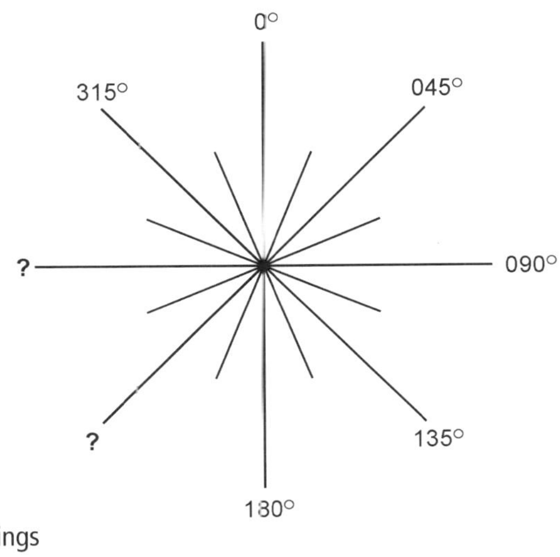

Figure 1.2 Grid bearings

Hint
In the examinations, compass directions and bearings on topographical maps are taken from grid north.

You are now going to use these two methods to give both the compass direction and the grid bearing of the Trigonometrical Station at 470735 from the Trigonometrical Station at 421809 on the Shamva map. Use the grid references to locate the two features on the map. See Figure 1.3 below.

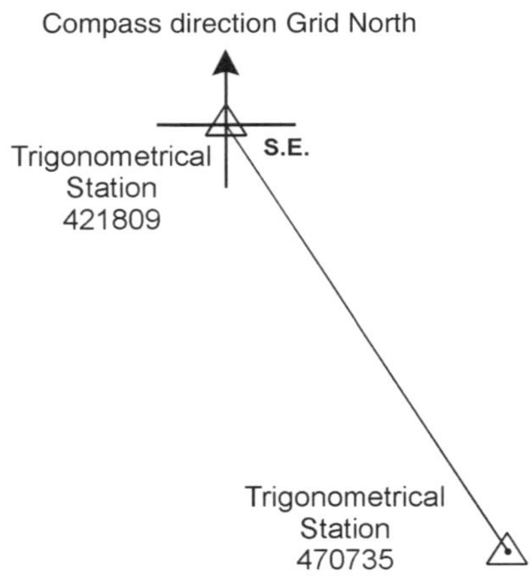

Figure 1.3

To give the compass direction of the Trigonometrical Station at 470735 from the Trigonometrical Station at 421809:

- Draw a straight line on the map between these two locations.
- Draw a line through the Trigonometrical Station at 421809 parallel to the eastings grid lines to show grid north.
- Through the Trigonometrical Station at 421809 also draw a line parallel to the northings grid lines.
- These two lines now enable you to give the compass direction of the Trigonometrical Station at 470735 from the Trigonometrical Station at 421809, namely south east.

To give the grid bearing of the Trigonometrical Station at 470735 from the Trigonometrical Station at 421809:

- Do exactly the same as described for giving the compass direction but use a protractor to measure the bearing in degrees from grid north. Always measure CLOCKWISE from grid north.

Glossary
CLOCKWISE – movement in the same direction as the hands of a clock

Note that east is 90° from grid north, south 180° from grid north and west 270° from grid north. This makes the measurement easier. In this case the bearing from grid north is 147°. (See Figure 1.4 below.)

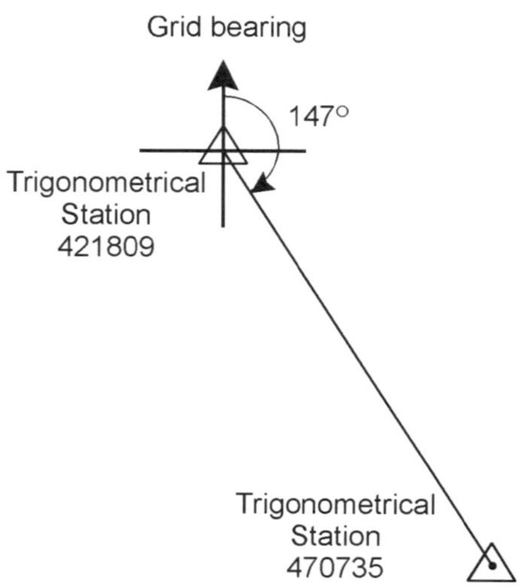

Figure 1.4

D Measuring distances

Maps are drawn to scale. The actual sizes of features on the ground and the distances between them can be reduced, in proportion, in order to show them on a topographical map. In this module, the scale of the Shamva map is 1:50 000, meaning that 1 unit on the map represents 50 000 of these units on the ground, in other words, 1 centimetre on the map represents 50 000 centimetres or 500 metres on the ground. Some maps, however, are drawn on a scale of 1:25 000. This means that 1 centimetre on the map represents 25 000 centimetres or 250 metres on the ground.

Distances on these maps are shown in three ways:

- by a statement in words for example, '2 centimetres represents 1 kilometre'
- by a representative fraction 1:50 000 or 1:25 000
- by a linear scale.

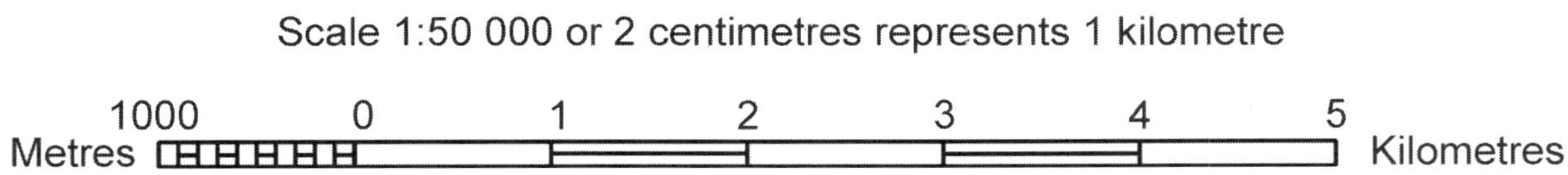

Figure 1.5 Three ways of showing distance on a map

How to measure a straight line distance

Refer to the Shamva map and locate the southern end of the embankment along the road at grid reference 477883. You are going to measure the distance along the road from this location to the road junction at grid reference 474865.

- Place a ruler or a straight edge of a piece of paper on the map and measure or mark off the distance along the road between these locations.
- Transfer this measurement to the scale line provided below the map.
- Read off the distance that this measurement represents. If the measurement extends beyond whole units of 1 kilometre, move your ruler or paper to one of the kilometre marks and use the divided kilometre on the left of the scale line. This gives divisions in 100 metre blocks. In this case the distance measured on the map is 3.5 centimetres which represents 1 kilometre and 750 metres or 1 750 metres.

Hint
Sometimes in examinations a clear instruction is given for a distance to be given in kilometres. At other times the distance is to be given in metres. Make sure you comply with the instruction given.

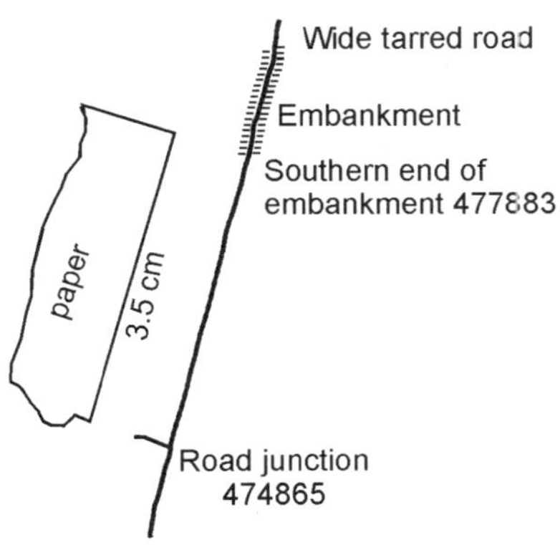

Figure 1.6 Measuring a straight line distance on a map

How to measure a curved distance

Again refer to the Shamva map to locate the road junction at grid reference 428741. You are going to measure the distance along the road from this road junction to the southern edge of the map at grid reference 422700.

- Divide the length of the (road) into straight sections.

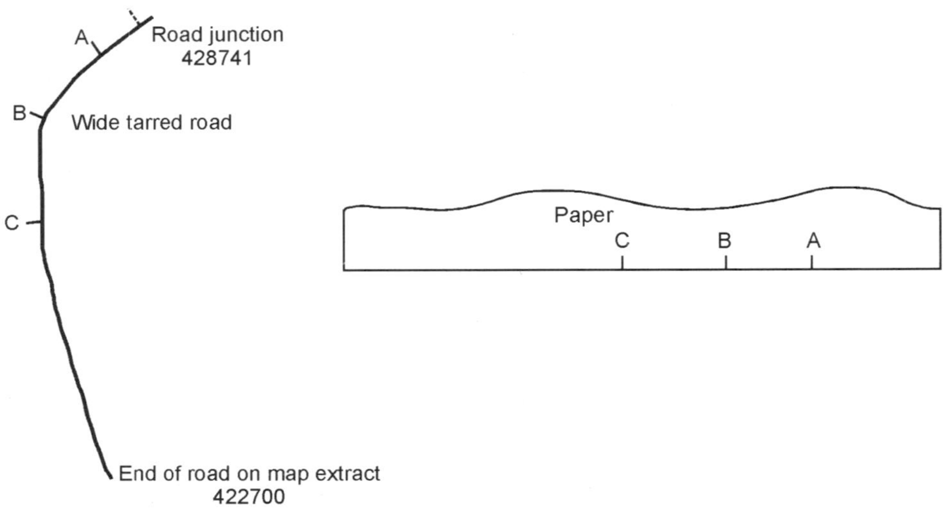

Figure 1.7 Measuring a curved distance on a map

- Place a corner of a straight edge of paper on the road junction at grid reference 428741 and mark on the paper the first bend in the road **A** as shown in Figure 1.7.
- Keeping the mark you have made for **A** firmly fixed, ROTATE the straight edge of paper until it follows the stretch of road from **A** to **B** – mark this point. Repeat this PROCEDURE for the stretches of road from **B** to **C** and from **C** to the end of the road at grid reference 422700.
- When you have completed the measurements lay the straight edge along the linear scale of the map and read off the total distance. The mark on the paper is 9.5 centimetres. This represents 4 kilometres 800 metres or 4 800 metres.

Glossary
ROTATE – move around a point
PROCEDURE – method

ACTIVITY 2

The answers are on page 23.

1 Complete Figure 1.1 and Figure 1.2 on page 3.

2 Look at the Shamva map and answer the following questions:

   a State the compass direction in which the River Mazowe flows.

   b What is the grid bearing of the reservoir at grid reference 486884 from the Trigonometrical Station at 505873?

   c Measure the straight line distance from the Trigonometrical Station at grid reference 470735 to the Trigonometrical Station at grid reference 421809.

E Determining heights

Heights are shown in three ways on topographical maps:

- **spot heights** are marked on maps as follows with the heights given in metres. The spot height in grid square 5385 on the Shamva map is 954.

The height of this point has been accurately measured. It is shown on the map but it is not shown by a feature on the ground.

- **trigonometrical stations** are shown on maps by the following symbol with the height given in metres, for example the Trigonometrical Station in grid square 5087 on the Shamva map

△ 1013.6

This is represented on the ground by a pillar and the height given is that of the top of this pillar.

- **contours** are lines joining places of the same height. They are shown on topographical maps as brown lines. They are not marked on the ground. The spacing between contours is known as the contour interval. Look at the key on the Shamva map; the contour interval is 20 metres. Here, only the contour lines representing each 100 metres are numbered. On 1:25 000 maps, however, the contour interval is 10 metres and so thicker contour lines are drawn every 100 metres.

F Calculating gradients

You can now use distance and height to calculate the steepness or gradient of a slope. Slopes differ in their steepness and you can determine just how steep a slope is by referring to height and distance details on a topographical map. The gradient is usually given as a ratio, for example, 1:10. This means that for every 10 units of horizontal distance on the ground you would ascend or descend by 1 unit.

Stages in calculating a gradient:

- find the difference in height between the two points
- measure the horizontal distance either as a straight line or a curved line (see **D Measuring distances** on page 5)
- make sure that you measure both differences in height and the horizontal distance **in the same units**, namely metres
- use this formula $\frac{\text{difference in height between the two points}}{\text{horizontal distance between the two points}}$

  and give the gradient as a ratio

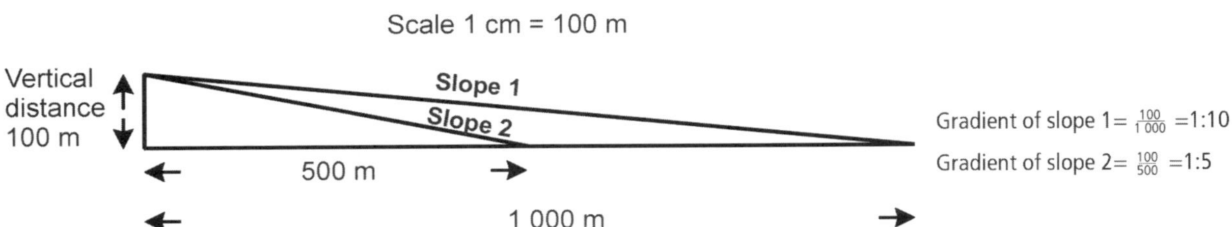

Figure 1.8 Calculating the gradient of a slope

ACTIVITY 3

Answers are on page 23.

Find the following grid references on the Shamva map – 453763 and 450788 to answer the following:

1 What is the value of each of the contours crossing the main road at each of these grid references?

2 What is the distance along the road between these two grid references?

3 Use the formula, given in section **F Calculating gradients**, to calculate the gradient along the road between these two grid references.

G Interpreting cross-sections

How to draw a cross-section

- Select a line on the map that you wish to show in a cross-section.
- Along this line place a piece of paper, marking on it where contours and significant physical features, such as a river, cross the line of section.
- On graph paper draw a base line the same length as the cross-section line and choose a vertical scale. Do not over-exaggerate the vertical scale. Write the scales selected alongside the vertical scale line and beneath the base line.
- Transfer the marks of contours and other physical features from the piece of paper to the base line of the section and with reference to the vertical scale, mark dots accordingly at equivalent heights on the section.
- Join up these dots with a smooth curve, naming any prominent features – hills, rivers, etc.

Hint
In the examination you will **not** be required to construct a cross-section. You may, however, be asked to annotate or interpret a cross-section presented. In an assignment submitted as part of coursework, you may wish to include cross-sections to illustrate features and show relationships between relief, drainage and land use features.

Interpreting a cross-section

When analysing a cross-section take note of variations in heights, slopes and shapes of prominent physical features. You may be required to add other details to a cross-section from the topographical map provided.

ACTIVITY 4

Answers are on page 23.

The cross-section below has been drawn along easting 45 between northing 83 and the northern edge of the Shamva map. Either make a copy of this cross-section using tracing paper or draw in pencil on the cross-section printed below:

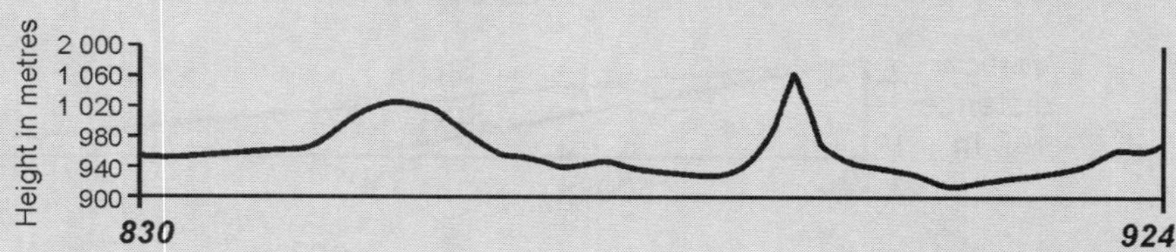

HIGHEST POINT ON THE SECTION	
Name	
Height	

1 Draw an arrow and label the locations of

a the River Mazowe

b a power line

c the railway.

2 **a** Print X on the highest point of the cross-section.

b In the spaces provided in the table next to the cross-section

i give the name of X

ii state its height in metres.

H Interpreting physical and human landscapes

You have learned how to extract details from topographical maps. It is now time to begin to interpret information included on these maps concerning both the physical and human landscapes shown.

A very important skill to acquire is that of being able to picture the physical landscape by using the contours on the map. They help you to interpret the shape of physical features. In addition you will learn how to use other map information, such as symbols, to understand relief and drainage features, coastal landscapes and natural vegetation.

Later in this section you will see how human features are shown on topographical maps and how human landscapes may be interpreted.

Interpreting physical landscapes

Relief features

Glossary
FORM – general shape and appearance

Contour patterns reveal much about the FORM of the **physical features** shown on a topographical map. It is important to be able to identify different types of slope and also to recognise some of the main features of a physical landscape.

Slopes may exist in a variety of forms. In Figure 1.9 the slope is both even and **gentle**. It is shown to be even because the contours are evenly spaced and because they are also widely spaced, the slope rises gradually.

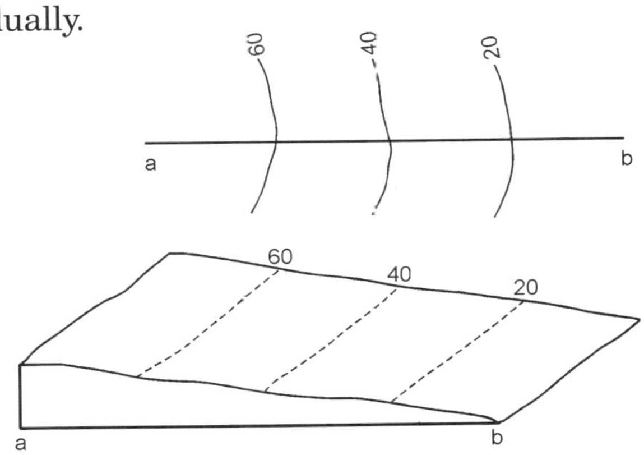

Figure 1.9 A gentle, even slope is shown by widely spaced contours

In Figure 1.10 the slope is again even but this time the contours are close together indicating a **steep** slope.

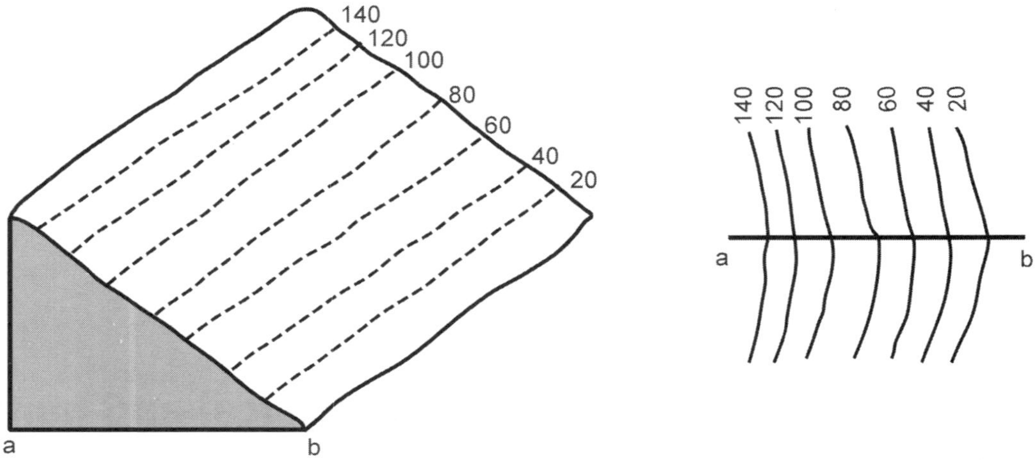

Figure 1.10 A steep, even slope is shown by contours that are close

In Figure 1.11 the lower part of the slope is gentle but with an increase in height the contours are seen to be closer together, indicating a steeper slope. This is known as a **concave** slope.

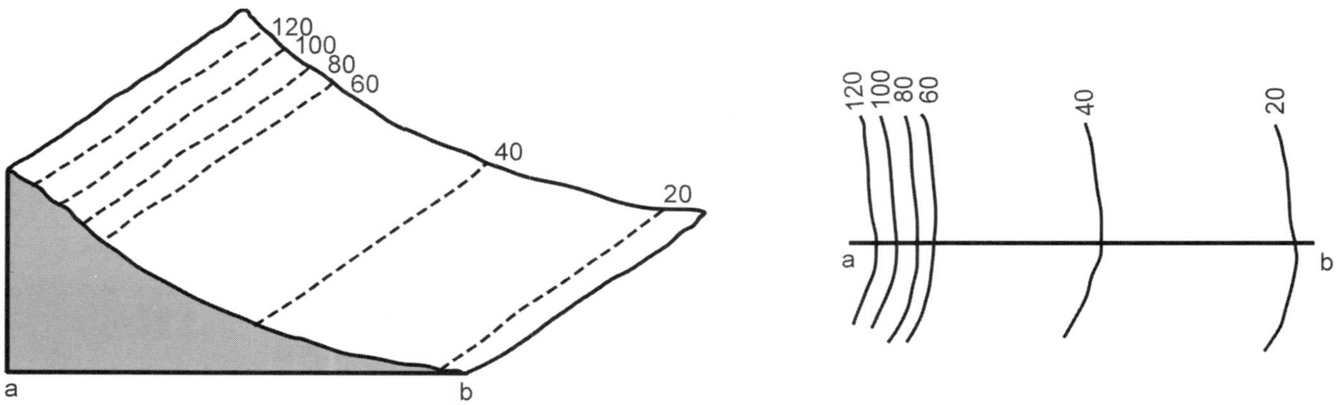

Figure 1.11 A concave slope

In Figure 1.12 contours become more widely spaced with an increase in height. This is referred to as a **convex** slope.

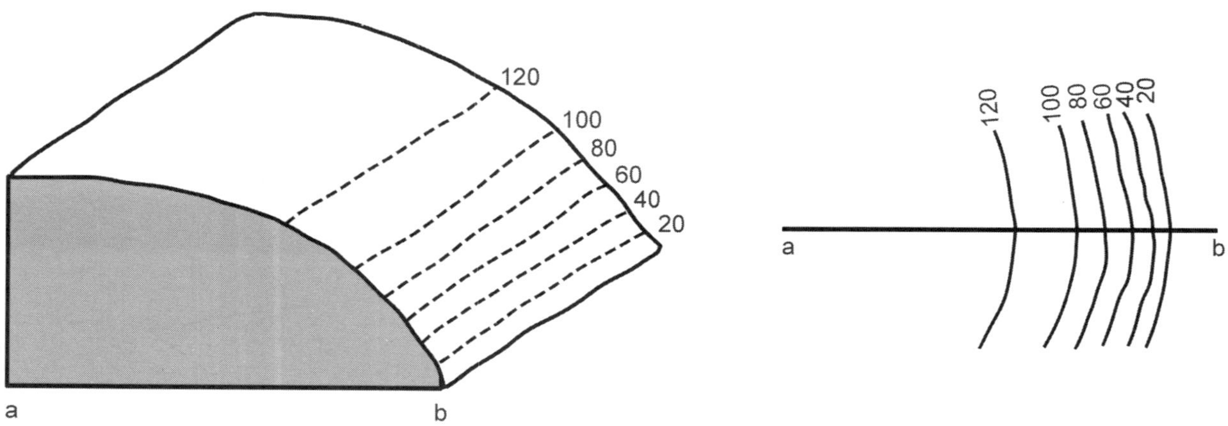

Figure 1.12 A convex slope

In Figure 1.13 contours are extremely close together. This shows a vertical or near vertical slope or **cliff**. On some topographical maps a cliff may be shown by symbol. Look at the key for the Shamva map to see how cliffs may be shown on the map.

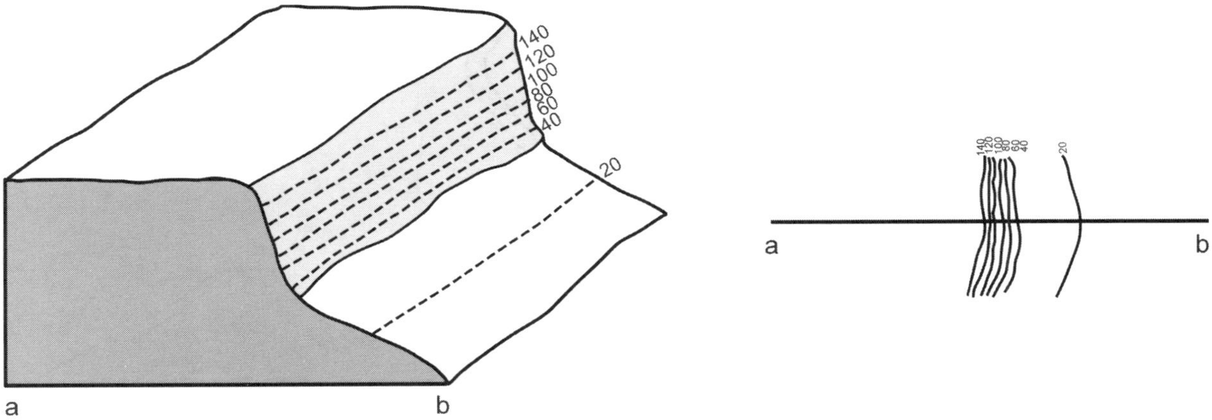

Figure 1.13 A nearly vertical slope or cliff

Having looked at different forms of slope we now can see how contours show relief features which may be present in the physical landscape. In Figure 1.14 we see a hill where the slope is similar in all directions. This is known as a **conical hill**.

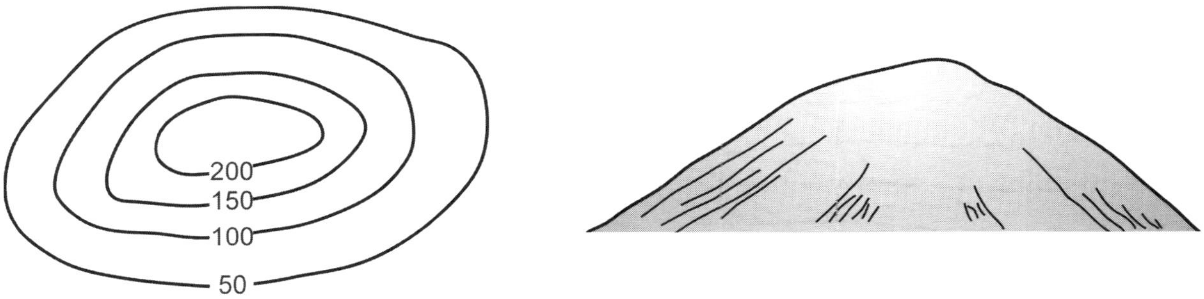

Figure 1.14 A conical hill

In Figure 1.15 an upland area is shown with steep sides. Here the contours are closely spaced. The top of the upland is shown to be level. This is known as a **plateau**.

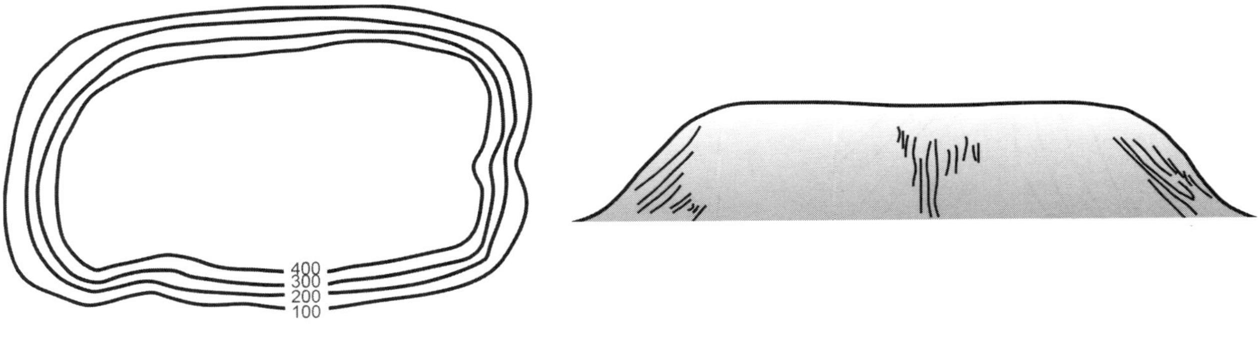

Figure 1.15 A plateau has steep sides

In Figure 1.16 a long narrow upland area is shown with steep sides. The contours are very close together and almost parallel to each other. This form of upland is called a **ridge**. There may be breaks in the ridge. A large break may be called a gap or pass.

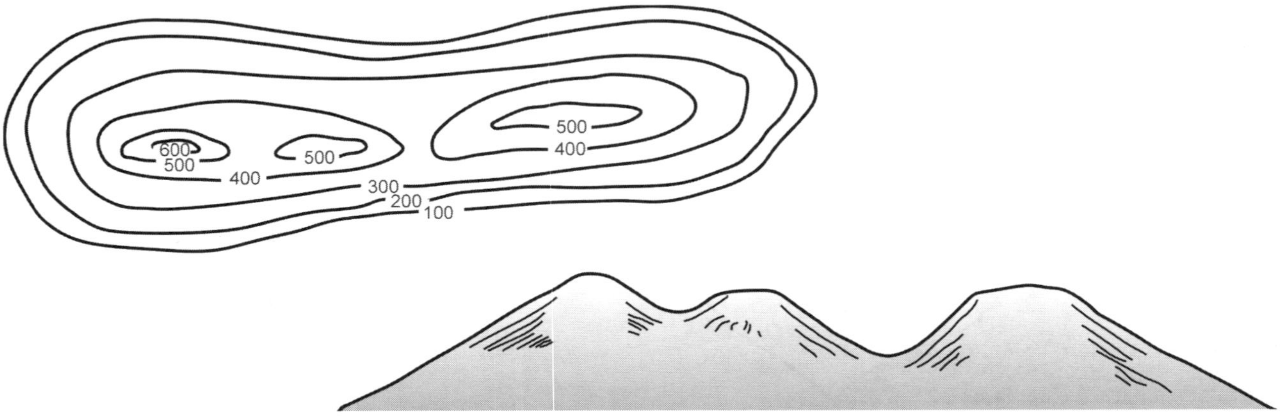

Figure 1.16 A ridge has steep sides and may have gaps or passes

In Figure 1.17 a narrow piece of upland is pointing into a lowland. This is a **spur**. Its contours are usually V-shaped and the V points towards the lowland.

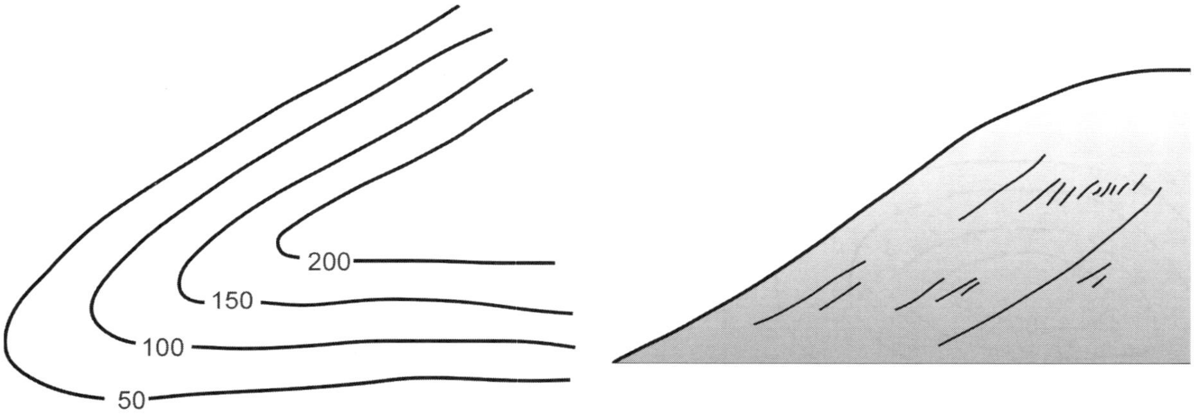

Figure 1.17 A spur has V-shaped contours that point towards lowland

In Figure 1.18 a **valley** is shown. This is a lowland between surrounding higher land areas. Contours in a valley are V-shaped. Here though the V points towards the higher land. A valley often contains a river.

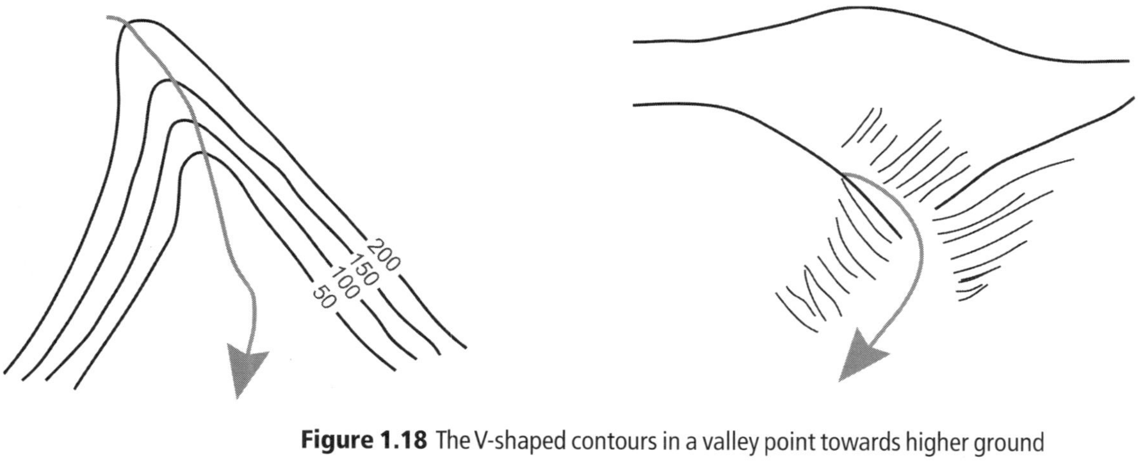

Figure 1.18 The V-shaped contours in a valley point towards higher ground

Figure 1.19 shows an upland with one steep slope (a scarp slope) and a gentle slope (a dip slope). This is known as an **escarpment**.

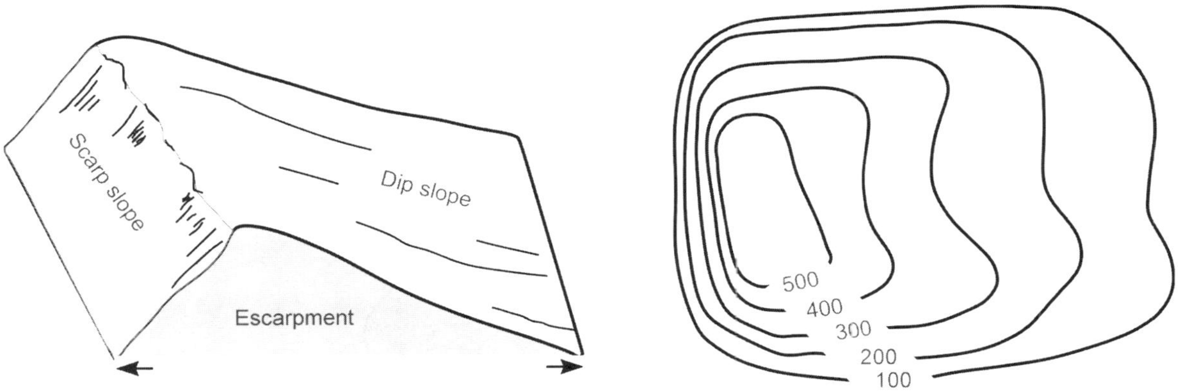

Figure 1.19 An escarpment has a scarp slope and a dip slope

Another descriptive term which is useful when interpreting the physical features shown on a topographical map is **plain**. This is a lowland, often flat or very gently sloping. Contours may either be absent or very widely spaced. A type of plain which often characterises large parts of some river valleys is a **flood plain**. This will be seen in the next part of this section when we look at drainage features.

Drainage features

Drainage features shown on a topographical map are shown in blue. Look at the key accompanying the Shamva map to see how different aspects of drainage are represented.

A **drainage basin** is the area drained by a river and its tributaries. The boundary of a drainage basin is known as a **watershed**. A line may be drawn on a map to show a watershed. This usually follows the crest of high land surrounding a drainage basin, see Figure 1.20.

The main features of the different parts of a drainage basin are summarised on page 15.

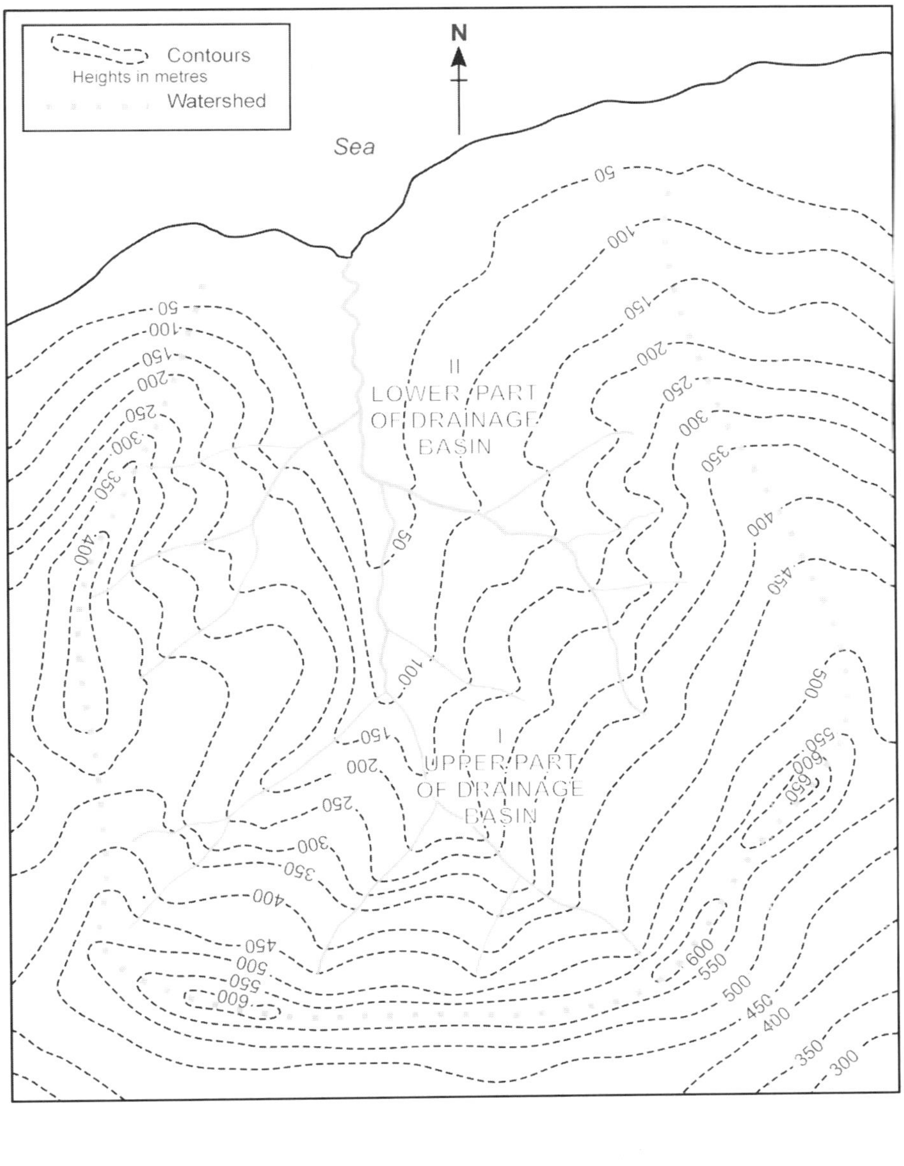

Figure 1.20 A contour sketch map showing some of the main features which characterise the different parts of a drainage basin

When looking at the pattern of drainage shown on a topographical map, you can often recognise one of the following three patterns: **dendritic**, **trellised** and **radial**. These are described in Figures 1.21, 1.22 and 1.23 below.

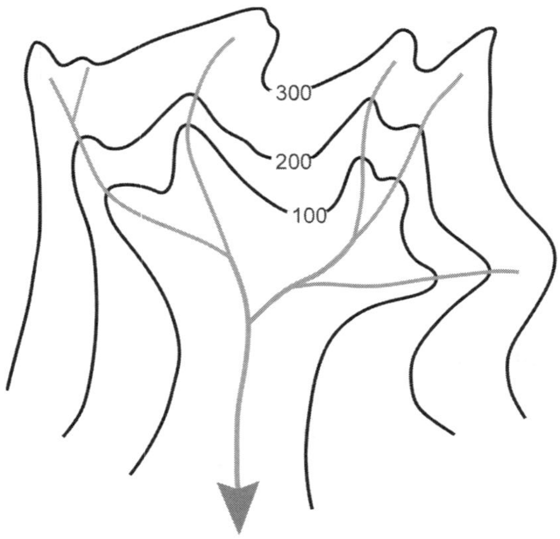

Figure 1.21 Dendritic drainage pattern. Tributaries join the main river at an acute angle. The overall pattern is like the branches of a tree.

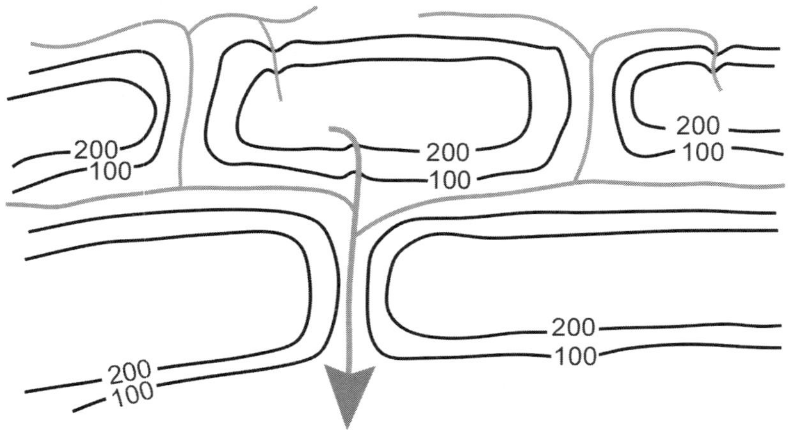

Figure 1.22 Trellised drainage pattern. Tributaries flow along areas of less resistant rock and join the main river at right angles.

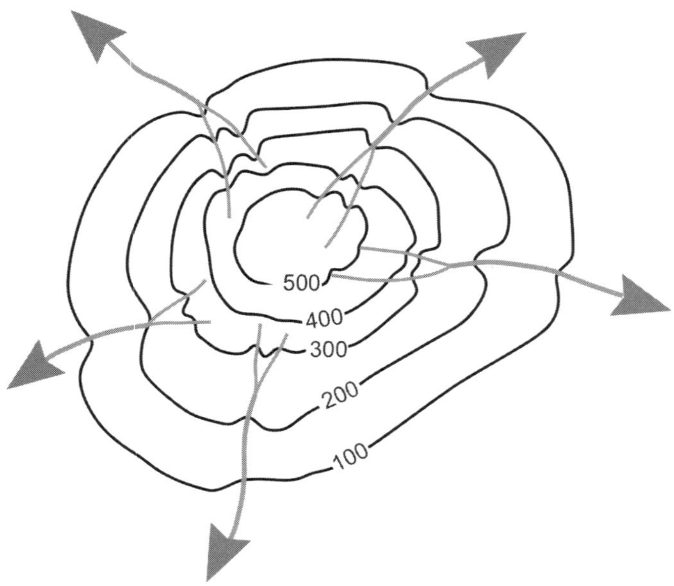

Figure 1.23 Radial drainage pattern. Rivers flow outward in all directions.

> **Hint**
> Drainage density is the length of rivers in relation to the size of an area.

Another feature of drainage which can be detected from a topographical map is **drainage density**. If there are many rivers in an area then the drainage may be described as high density. Very few streams in an area may be described as low density.

From studies you have already made in Unit 4 of Module 2, you should be able to recognise some of the main river features shown on large-scale maps. Waterfalls and rapids are shown by symbols on the maps you will use. Other river features such as meanders, ox-bow lakes, flood plains and deltas can be clearly recognised on these maps. One additional feature which you may see on maps of some areas are islands in a river channel. These are sometimes called **eyots**. The river process is known as **braiding**, when islands are formed by deposition in a river channel. Look at the maps you have to see how many of these features you can identify.

> **Hint**
> If you are unsure about some of the physical features mentioned look back to Unit 4 of Module 2.

Figure 1.20 on page 13 is a contour sketch map showing some of the main features which characterise the different parts of a drainage basin, these are summarised below.

I The upper part of the drainage basin

valley features

- valleys are narrow, steep-sided and V-shaped in cross-section *(contours on the valley sides are close together. They point upstream to the higher land)*
- valley floors have steep gradients *(contours crossing the valley floors are close together)*

river features

- many headstreams (tributaries)
- rivers occupy most of the valley floor
- rivers flow around interlocking spurs
- rapids and waterfalls
- rivers have small volumes and flow in small channels

II The lower part of the drainage basin

valley features

- the main valley is wider
- valley sides are less steep *(contours are lower than in the upper part of the drainage basin and are more widely spaced)*
- much of the floor of the main valley may be level – a flood plain – and have a gentle gradient, especially nearer to the sea *(fewer contours crossing the valley floor)*

river features

- the main river channel is wider and does not occupy the whole of the valley floor
- meanders are more prominent
- ox-bow lakes and levees may be present
- some rivers may have deltas with distributaries at their mouths

ACTIVITY 5

Answers are on page 23.

Look at the Shamva map and answer the following questions:

1 Describe the physical feature shown by the contours around grid reference 435840.

2 State the type of slope in grid square 4382.

3 For the area defined by eastings 55 and 57 and northings 87 and 89, state the drainage pattern shown.

4 a What type of physical feature is shown in the area bounded by eastings 46 and 49 and northings 76 and 79?

  b Give a name to the slope facing to the north west.

  c Give a name to the slope facing to the south east.

  d Which of these two slopes has the greatest number of rivers flowing down it?

5 State the type of relief feature extending in a north easterly direction from Masimbe in grid square 4773.

Coastal features

As with river and drainage features, Unit 4 of Module 2 gives detail on marine processes and coastal features. Some of the coastal features may be seen on a topographical map. Some of those which may be represented are cliffs, wave-cut platforms, stacks, bay and headland coastlines, beaches, spits, bars, coastal sand dunes and marsh.

ACTIVITY 6

Answers are on page 24.

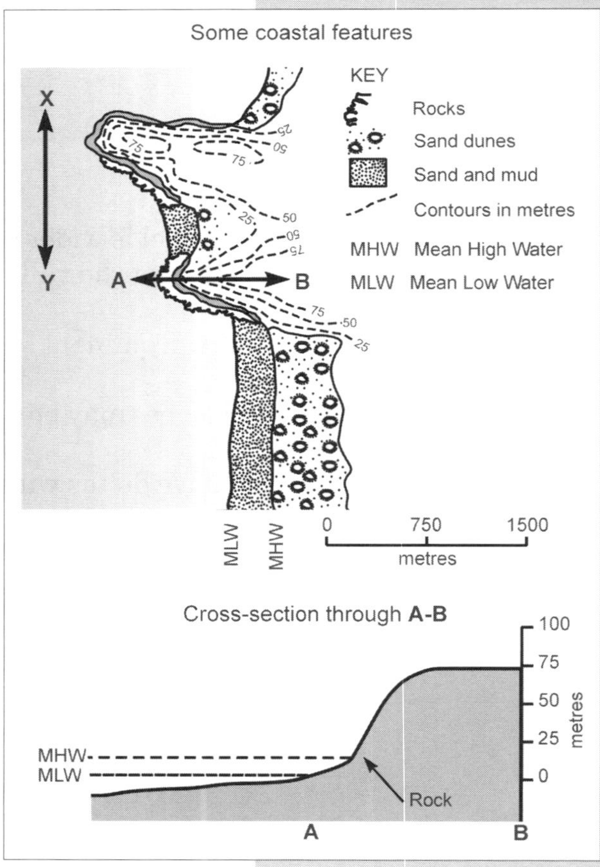

To revise your knowledge of some of these coastal features, study Figure 1.24. This shows a contour sketch map of a stretch of coastline together with a cross-section across part of the area.

Answer the following questions.

1 Describe the shape of the coastline from **X – Y**, naming the main coastal features shown.

2 Look at the cross-section **A – B** and describe the form of the coastline.

3 Measure the widest extent of sand dunes in the southern part of the coastline shown.

Figure 1.24 A contour sketch map and section

Natural vegetation

To determine the type and importance of **natural vegetation** shown on a topographical map, reference needs to be made to the **key** provided. Details of the extent of forest, other tree distributions, types of bush and scrub, the presence of swamp vegetation, including mangrove, may be seen by map study. It is sometimes possible to suggest reasons for the presence of certain types of vegetation in relation to physical features. For example, swamp vegetation usually characterises areas which are low lying and ill-drained.

Human activities may have a strong influence upon the extent of natural vegetation found in an area. It may have been cleared away to allow for cultivation or other developments. Natural vegetation may be confined to certain areas on a map. These could be areas which are physically unsuitable for development or are too isolated.

Interpreting human landscapes

It is evident when looking at a large-scale topographical map that many of the features displayed belong to the human landscape. People develop areas in different ways and so the characteristics of the human landscape may vary greatly from one area to another. Map study helps you to appreciate this. You must firstly recognise the nature of the human landscape by studying the key to the map and relating the symbols shown to the map itself.

Note: the symbols differ on maps of various countries. For example, the Shamva map is an area in Zimbabwe shown on a scale of 1:50 000. The symbols for this map would differ from a map of Mauritius, for example, that might be on a scale of 1:25 000.

Hint
A key will always be provided with the large-scale topographical map presented in the examination. However, some familiarity with the symbols enables you to interpret a map more easily.

ACTIVITY 7

Answers are on page 24.

1 On the Shamva map, look carefully at the symbols for each of the following and write a brief description of each symbol.

a areas of cultivation
b power lines
c tracks
d a railway
e built-up areas of a settlement.

2 What is the contour VERTICAL INTERVAL on the Shamva map?

3 With reference to the Shamva map and the photograph, state three features in square 4275 that are shown in the photograph.

Glossary
VERTICAL INTERVAL – the difference in height between one contour and the next contour

You now need to use your ability to identify map features relating to the human landscape to look for patterns and relationships. A summary of these is given in Figure 1.25 below. This shows that the main features of the human landscape are concerned with settlements, communications and other land-uses. Let us consider each of these features in turn and let us illustrate with reference to evidence shown on the Shamva map. Patterns and relationships will be the main themes of your map studies here.

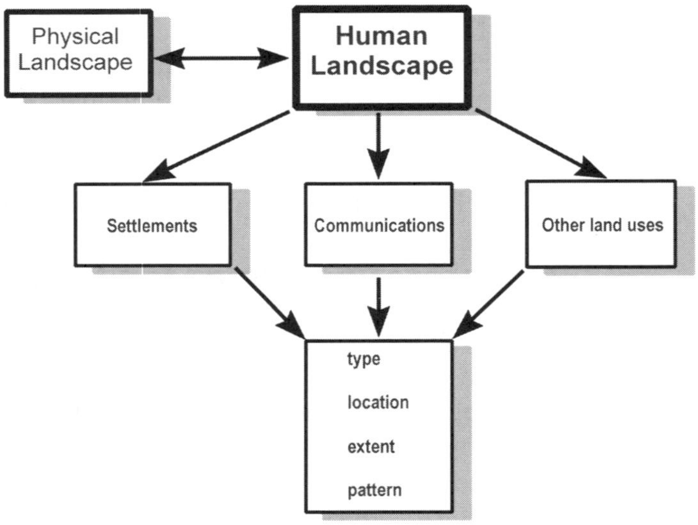

Figure 1.25 Characteristics of the human landscape and its relationship with the physical landscape

Glossary
SETTLEMENT – a place where people live (settle) permanently
RURAL SETTLEMENT – a settlement where most of the people are engaged in primary activities, such as farming
URBAN SETTLEMENT – a built-up area where most of the population live and are engaged in secondary activities such as manufacturing as well as services, it spreads out more than a rural settlement
SITE – the ground on which a settlement is found
SITUATION – position of a settlement in relation to other features and settlements
FUNCTIONS – activities of people in a settlement
SETTLEMENT PATTERNS – the arrangement (spacing) of settlements in an area
DISPERSED – scattered buildings
LINEAR – buildings arranged along a line such as a road or river
NUCLEATED – a settlement where buildings are close together
URBAN MORPHOLOGY – the pattern or shape of a built-up area

Hint
Interpretation must at all times be supported by map evidence.

Settlement

You need to refer to Unit 3 of Module 1 to revise your ideas on the differences between RURAL SETTLEMENT and URBAN SETTLEMENT. At the same time you should be familiar with the meaning of SITE, SITUATION and FUNCTIONS of settlements and with factors influencing these characteristics. You need to understand SETTLEMENT PATTERNS – DISPERSED, LINEAR and NUCLEATED, as well as features of URBAN MORPHOLOGY. This is a good example of the advantages of studying topographical maps at the same time as you work through the content of Modules 1–3.

To illustrate some of the settlement features which may be determined from a study of topographical maps, let us look at the Shamva map.

You can start by trying to identify the services offered by the settlement of Shamva. From symbols given on the map you can see evidence of a number of services – a hospital, a post office, a police station, District Administration Office, an aerodrome landing area, a railway, services such as sewage and water supply (reservoirs), as well as leisure facilities such as a sports field and rifle range.

Map evidence may reveal **patterns of settlement** and you may be able to suggest reasons for the distribution of settlements or the absence of settlement in an area. On the Shamva map there are some huts to the south east of the River Nyagui in the area named Mangwende Communal Land. You are now going to try to describe the pattern of settlement shown by these huts. From map evidence, you can see that many of the huts are on or near to cultivated land.

There are few huts or none in the areas of bush. Huts are found near tracks or roads however. They are found on gently sloping land and lower land avoiding steep slopes and high land. Try to suggest reasons for this pattern of distribution.

Sometimes map-reading questions require you to describe the **site** or **situation** of a settlement and to suggest reasons for its growth. Again you can take an example from the Shamva map. The question you should consider is – What does the map suggest about the site, situation and reasons for the growth of the settlement of Shamva itself?

You can see immediately that the settlement is sited on gently sloping land. Water supply is readily available from a number of reservoirs. Its growth appears to be mainly concerned with the development of mining in the area a few kilometres to the south of the settlement. It also acts as a communications centre for the area. There is a railway connection to the west. Shamva also lies close to the main north-south road running through the area. It lies near to the meeting point of this main road and a narrow road from the west. There is an aerodrome landing area close to the settlement.

ACTIVITY 8

Answers are on page 24.

Study the Shamva map and answer the following questions about settlements shown on the map.

1 Describe the type of settlement at each of the following locations and suggest its main function:

a square 4184

b square 4784.

2 **a** Describe the pattern of settlement at Nyagui (square 5671).

b What evidence suggests the Nyagui serves a wider rural area?

Communications

Movement of people and goods is a vital feature of human activity. Maps give a clear indication of major lines of such movements by the presence of roads and railways. Other forms of communication may be located in an area, as evidenced for example by the presence of an airfield / airport or a ferry service. In rural areas, where more people travel on foot, tracks have a significant role to play as an essential part of local communications.

In addition to the type of communications present, a topographical map also reveals the density of communications.

- Is there a dense or a sparse network of communications in an area?
- Are some parts of the map area lacking in communications?

You can use map information to help you to suggest reasons why these characteristics may occur. The physical landscape may exert a strong influence on communications. Routes frequently follow low lying areas such as plains or valley floors. Where these favourable physical features meet, communications may CONVERGE. This may help to explain why certain settlements become important as route centres.

Glossary
CONVERGE – meet

Communications may be absent in some areas where the physical background presents difficulties of construction, such as steep slopes and upland areas, as well as regions which are ill-drained. People may overcome these physical difficulties, however, by constructing embankments, cuttings and tunnels, as well as draining land. Airfields require particular physical conditions; try to work out what these are.

Features of the human landscape may also play an important role in determining the location and density of communications networks. These include the size and density of settlements and the degree of economic development in an area, for example, mining and farming.

Main land uses shown on large-scale maps

These include a number of different illustrations, the most important being agriculture, mining, industry, power production, water supply, forestry and tourist attractions. On some maps one or more of these land uses may be very significant in the human landscape.

- **Agricultural land use**

Glossary
CULTIVATION – growing crops
PASTORAL – keeping of animals
IRRIGATED – supplying extra water to the land
ESTATE or PLANTATION – large area growing specialist crops

Agricultural land may be used for a variety of purposes – it may be used for the CULTIVATION of crops or for PASTORAL purposes.
In some instances agricultural land may be IRRIGATED. Reference to the map key can help you to identify the use made of agricultural land. You will notice differences in defining agricultural land. More detail about the specific uses of some of the cultivated land, for example, types of ESTATE or PLANTATION, is given on the map of Shamva.

It will help you to see how map evidence may be used to describe agricultural land use if you use the Shamva map as an illustration.

Large areas of cultivation are shown, especially in the north west sector of the map and in the south east. Smaller patches are located elsewhere. In large areas of the map, however, bush rather than cultivated land is present. You can see that the cultivated areas tend to be where the lower and more level land is found. These areas usually have a number of rivers flowing through them suggesting that the land is well drained and so is suitable for cultivation. Some of the rivers may supply water for the crops.

Hint
If in the examination you are asked to describe the land uses in a defined area of the map – you should include all the land uses you see. If the question excludes certain land uses, then ***do not*** include these in your answer. You will be wasting time if you do and will not receive any credit for this information.

You can also see that cultivated land is absent from steep slopes, especially in the central part of the map area. Orchards or plantations (note that they are grouped together in the key) are located in small patches, for example in grid squares 5191, 5589 and 5689. Dip tanks, as at grid reference 517808, suggest pastoral farming. Irrigated farming is evidenced by the presence of canals in the north east of the map area, for example in grid square 5091 and reservoirs as for instance in grid square 5590.

- **Land used for mining**

Glossary
MINE DUMPS – mounds of waste rock as a result of mining
MINING TRENCHES – a long narrow cut in the ground – made when looking for minerals
EXCAVATIONS – large hollows made in the ground when rock has been taken away during mining

Some map extracts include areas where mining is an important activity. On the map of Shamva, mining areas are located close to the settlement of Shamva. Evidence of mining on this map is shown by the names of mines such as Shamva Mine A in grid squares 4784 and 4884. Other mining features shown on the map include MINE DUMPS, for example in grid squares 4785 and 4885, MINING TRENCHES as in the southern part of grid square 4985 and EXCAVATIONS as along the ridge TSAMVI in grid squares 4784 and 4884.

Water for mining will be obtained from the headstreams draining into the large reservoir in grid square 5187, as well as from smaller reservoirs. Communications serving the mine include the main north-south road and the road leading westwards from Shamva together with the railway. Power lines provide the necessary power needed for mining activities.

Summary

A In the first section you looked at the key role played by symbols in conveying a great deal of useful information on topographical maps. A key feature of successful map reading is the ability to translate map symbols into actual features.

B To locate specific features on maps it is necessary to use grid lines and to be able to give and read both four-figure and six-figure grid references.

C It is fundamental to be able to give directions on maps. Directions are given either with reference to compass points or as grid bearings from grid north.

D All maps are drawn to scale. You need to be familiar, for instance, with the difference between a 1:50 000 topographical map and one drawn to the scale of 1:25 000. You looked at how both straight line distances and curved distances could be measured.

E All topographical maps show height by making use of spot heights, heights shown against trigonometrical stations and contour lines.

F Having studied the measurement of distance and the determination of height, you looked in this section to how both of these could be used to calculate the gradient of a slope.

G To appreciate map details from a different perspective, a line of section may be drawn across part of the map and a profile or cross-section drawn. This allows you to see both the relative heights along the line selected and slope details. You can also use a cross-section to locate features shown on the map in their correct position.

H After becoming familiar with the mechanics of map reading, the final section looked at ways in which map information may be interpreted. Essentially an area is made up of a physical landscape with details of relief and drainage. Superimposed upon this background is the human landscape with information as to how people have developed an area. Different land uses may be described from a topographical map including settlement, communications and other land uses. Relationships between the physical and the human landscape and between different aspects of the human landscape may be determined using map evidence.

Check your progress

Study the Shamva map

1 Give the six-figure grid reference of the footbridge on the wide tarred road bridge as it crosses the River Mazowe. [1]

2 Use map evidence to describe three ways in which mining to the south of Shamva has caused visual pollution. [3]

3 Describe the River Nyagui in the south east of the map area.

In your answer

a state the direction of flow, [1]

b the main features of the river channel. [4]

4 Name the land use located:

a at grid reference 435819,

b in grid square 4184 and named in grid square 4284. [2]

5 **a** Give the grid square reference for Rutherdale Reservoir about 2 km to the south of Shamva Station. [1]

b Suggest two reasons for its location. [2]

6 Why is there little settlement in the area marked Grahamsdale to the south of northing 82 in the eastern part of the area shown on the map? [3]

Feedback to activities

FEEDBACK 1

1 Tsamvi.

2 The Carse Estate.

3 Hospital.

4 954 m.

5 Dip tank.

FEEDBACK 2

1 Figure 1.1: WNW and ENE

Figure 1.2: 225° and 270°

2 **a** Eastwards / from west to east.

b 300°.

c 8 km 900 m / 8 900 m.

FEEDBACK 3

1 Contour at 453763 = 1 060 m.

Contour at 450788 = 1 020 m.

2 2 600 m.

3 $$\frac{40}{2\,600} = 1{:}65$$

Note 40 m is the difference in height, 2 600 m is the distance between the contours. Gradient given as a ratio.

FEEDBACK 4

Here is the completed section.

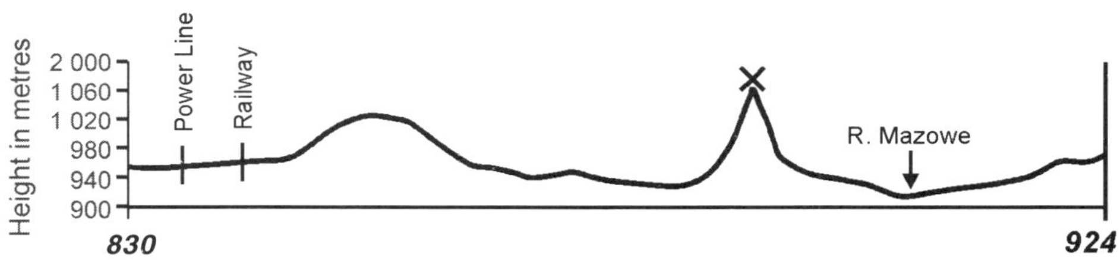

HIGHEST POINT ON THE SECTION	
Name	Chipiso
Height	1 060 m

FEEDBACK 5

1 Conical hill.

2 Concave slope.

3 Radial drainage.

4 **a** escarpment

b scarp slope

c dip slope

d scarp slope.

5 Ridge.

FEEDBACK 6

1 indented / irregular

headlands, cliffs, wave-cut platform, bay, beach, sand dunes.

2 steep slope above the MHW (mean high water level).

3 width 1.1 cm

scale on diagram 1 cm = 500 m

1.1 cm = 550 m.

FEEDBACK 7

1 **a** light brown shading

b red line

c broken red line

d black / white blocks

e grey shading.

2 The vertical interval is 20 metres.

3 Three features shown on the map and in the photograph are:

smooth rock, medium bush, building.

You will note that where the cattle are grazing coincides with an area described as 'cultivation' in the key to the map. Cultivation can mean farming in general, whether arable (crops) or pastoral (animal).

FEEDBACK 8

1 **a** nucleated – agricultural estate.

b linear – mine camp.

2 **a** There is a linear arrangement of huts along gravel roads.

b Roads and tracks converge; there is a school at Nyagui.

Unit 2
The representation and interpretation of data

Geographers make use of data presented in a variety of forms. You need to be conversant with a variety of techniques of presenting information. In this unit, ways in which you can present information in a clear, concise and appropriate form are considered. You will be provided with guidelines on how to construct graphs, maps and diagrams from data provided. In addition, you will practise analysing and interpreting data from a number of different presentations including graphs, maps, diagrams, statistics and tables of data, photographs and pictorial materials, as well as written accounts.

Interpretation of data, however presented, is a very important feature of all geography examination papers. We hope that what follows in Unit 2 will help you to gain confidence in using these techniques and you can also use them for Unit 3. Practise using them frequently. In time you will become familiar with how they are constructed, what they can tell you and how they can help you to understand the subject more clearly.

This unit is divided into the following sections:

A	Graphs
B	Maps
C	Diagrams
D	Photographic and pictorial material
E	Tables of data
F	Written accounts

When you have finished this unit you should be able to:

- present data in a variety of forms
- select the most appropriate ways of presenting data
- interpret a range of presentation techniques
- translate data from one presentation technique to another
- recognise patterns and relationships in data.

A Graphs

Geographers use a large number of statistics. By themselves, statistics do not always give you a clear pattern. It is only when statistics are converted to other forms of presentation, such as graphs, that you can begin to see the importance of the data. There are a number of types of graphs that you will become familiar with.

Each type has its uses and you are going to see how they are constructed and interpreted. The types of graphs you are going to be concerned with are:

- line graphs
- pie graphs
- bar graphs, including divided bar graphs
- triangular graphs
- radial graphs
- scatter graphs
- compound line graphs.

Line graphs

Hint
The x axis often shows dates, time or distance.
The y axis often shows size or frequency.

Line graphs have two axes.

- One axis is **horizontal** and is known as the **x axis**.
- The other axis is **vertical** and is known as the **y axis**.

In the graph below (Figure 2.1) dates are shown from 1750 to 2100 on the x axis. The y axis shows population in billions.

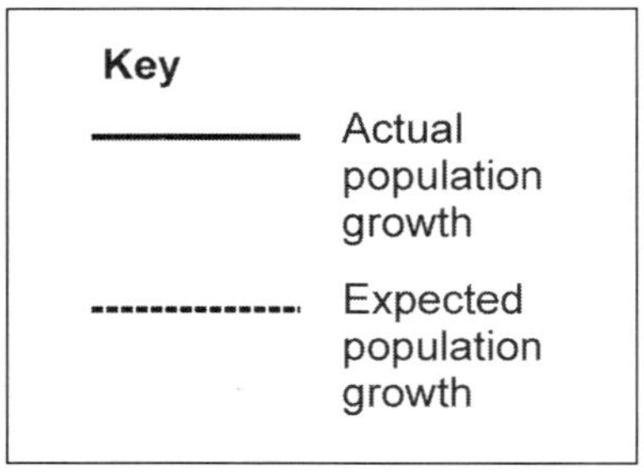

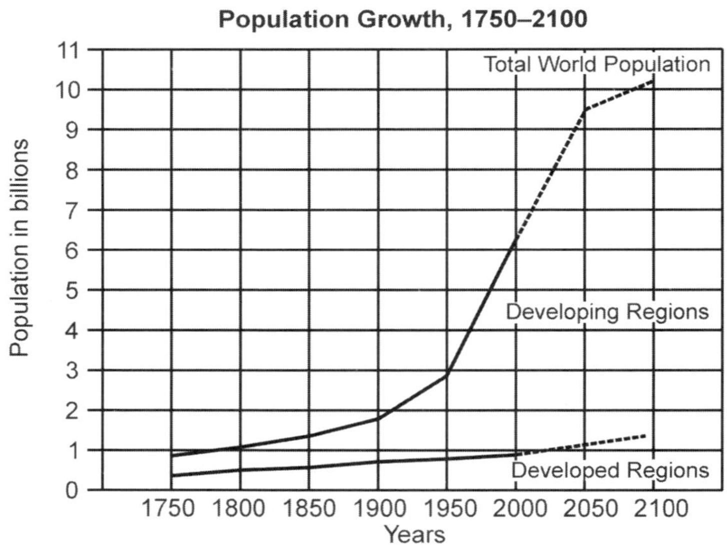

Figure 2.1 Population growth, 1750–2100

Stages in the construction of a line graph

- It is important that you choose a suitable **scale** for each axis. It is a good idea to consider how much space you have available on your page before you decide on the scale you will use. Find the highest and lowest values for each and relate the lengths of the axes to these values.
- You will notice in the graph above that we show different years between 1750 and 2100. The population data you have is for every 50 years. You need to mark even spaces along the x axis to represent these blocks of time. In the same way, we are attempting to show population growth from below 1 billion to over 10 billion on the y axis. Having decided on a scale again, you need to clearly mark 0 to 11 billion at even spaces along the y axis.

Hint
The x axis shows constant values, the y axis shows changing values.

- Each axis needs to be clearly labelled, including the units used. In this case the axes are 'years' and 'population in billions'. When you plot time intervals along the x axis always make sure that you divide the axis into equal divisions.
- Each point is plotted on the graph with a value for each of the axes.
- When these values are plotted they can be joined with a line. You are advised to draw the line with a pencil.
- Always write a title for a graph.

How to read a line graph

- When the graph is complete, you are now in a position to see trends shown by the line you have drawn. For example, how long it took for the population to increase by a billion (Fig 2.1). When was growth most rapid (shown by a steepening of the line)?
- Look for a TREND. In Figure 2.2 the line fluctuates greatly from year to year but the arrow shows the general trend.

Glossary
TREND – pattern

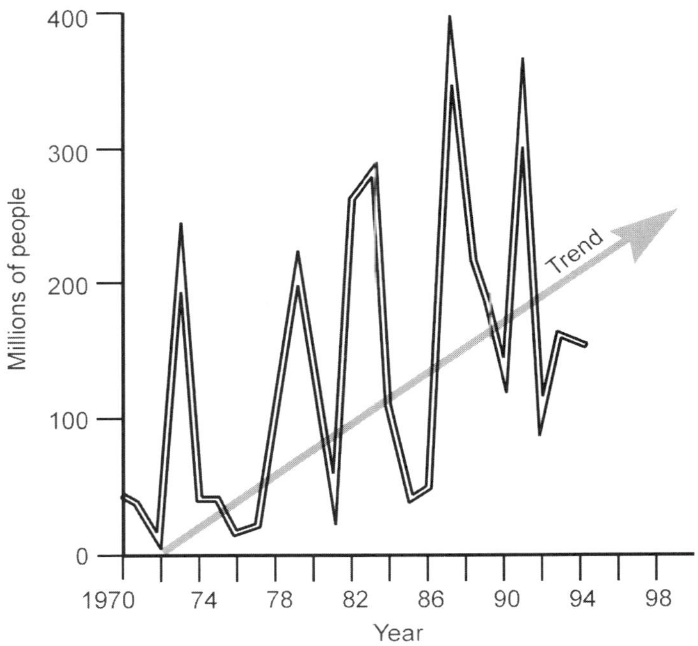

Figure 2.2 Number of people affected by natural hazards

Uses of line graphs

- To show values over a given time such as temperatures, population or production figures.

Pie graphs

- A pie graph is a circle divided into segments or parts. These segments show at a glance their relative importance.
- The size of the circle does not matter if you are *only* concerned with comparing the contributions made by the parts making up the total.

Stages in the construction of a pie graph

> **Hint**
> Check your calculations for all the segments by adding them together. They should add up to 360°.

- Calculate the size of the segments in degrees.

  Use the formula

  $$\text{angle required in degrees} = \frac{\text{size of segment} \times 360^\circ}{\text{size of total}}$$

- Draw the first segment in the circle, using a protractor, by measuring from the start line. The next segment will be measured from the line you have just drawn. Always work in a clockwise direction, as shown by the arrow outside the circle in the example below. Measure and draw in the other segments until the pie graph is completed.
- Shade or colour the segments and provide a key.
- Give your pie graph a title.

To portray each of these stages reference may be made to Figure 2.3 below. Here you can see a completed pie graph showing how aid was spent on a part of Italy in 1955. The data upon which this pie graph was constructed is also given below in Table 1.

Notice that marks and values in percentages are given on the circle for every 10%. This enables you to complete the segments more easily. The marks have been made every 36° (100% = 360° therefore 10% = 36°). Starting with the largest segment , the amount of aid spent on farming, you can see from the data that it was 68%. From the start line (marked on Figure 2.3) you can look for 68% on the circle and draw a radius. The size of the next largest segment, 14% of aid spent on communications, is then added by measuring from the radius just drawn. In total so far 82% of the aid spending has been shown by these two segments. The remaining three segments have been drawn with reference to the data.

> **Hint**
> All of the segments in the pie graph are then shaded using the key provided.

Table 1

Percentage aid spent on	1955	A recent year
Communications	14	8
Farming	68	21
Industry	7	49
Water supply	10	12
Others	1	10

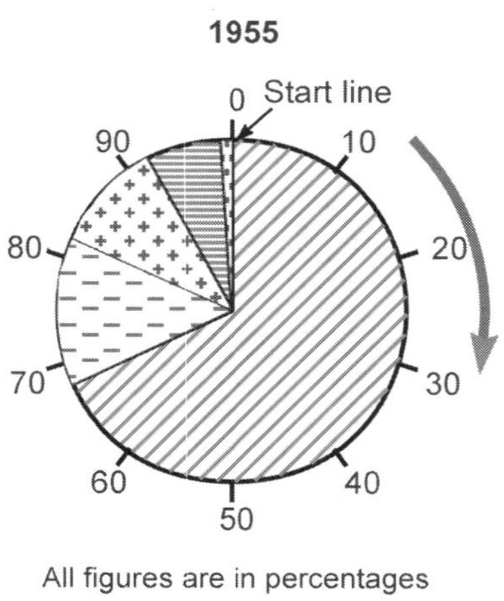

Figure 2.3 Aid spent on part of Italy in 1955

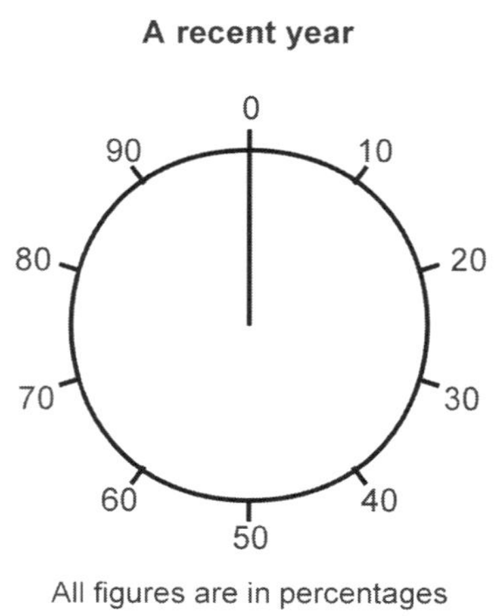

Figure 2.4 Aid spent on part of Italy in a recent year

ACTIVITY 1

Answers are on page 54.

From the data given in Table 1 for 'A recent year' on the previous page, construct a pie graph using the circle given in Figure 2.4. Use a pencil to draw the segments and to shade them. Use the key provided.

How to read a pie graph

- Look at the key to see what shading or colour has been used for each of the segments.
- A pie graph gives an instant picture as to the contribution that each segment makes to the total. It is worth remembering that each quarter of the circle represents 90°.

If you need to draw two or more circles using percentages, the circle sizes will be the same. However, if you attempt to show different totals using actual numbers rather than percentages, then you need to do a further calculation. This is to determine the radius of each circle and therefore the circle size. The radius of each circle is found by finding the square root of each total. This may be obtained by using a calculator. If two circles are to be drawn to represent totals of 400 and 900, the square roots will be 20 and 30.

The two circles could then be drawn with radii of 20 mm and 30 mm. This would make sure that the area of each circle is proportional to the different totals. The circles can then be divided into segments as explained above.

Uses of pie graphs

- To show the importance of parts in making up the total in one or more sets of data.

Bar graphs

- Bars on these graphs show different sizes or frequencies of distribution.

Hint
This bar graph shows the number and types of natural hazards experienced in the world in a recent year.

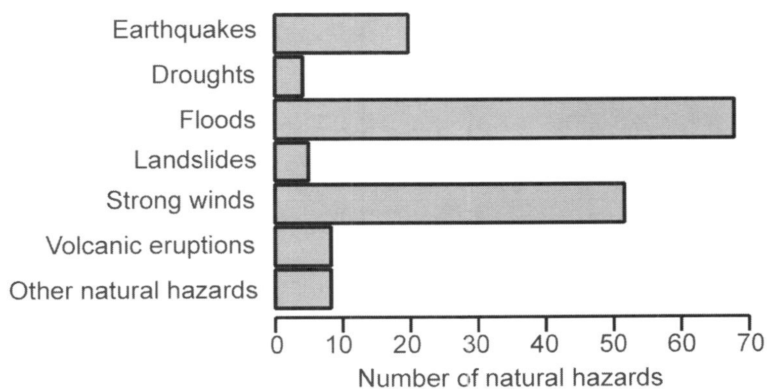

Figure 2.5 Number of natural hazards worldwide in a recent year

Stages in the construction of a bar graph

Hint
Note the range of values (the highest and the lowest) in deciding upon the scale.

- Show the values you wish to use on a vertical or horizontal scale.
- Draw bars next to each other along a base line, making them equal in width.

Divided bar graphs are used to show the contribution of parts. In Figure 2.6 below, bars have been divided to show the structure of the working population in two countries in the developed world and two countries in the developing world. These bars have been drawn horizontally but they can be presented vertically.

> **Hint**
> Divided bar graphs are also referred to as divided rectangles.

Other types of bar graph are shown below (Figures 2.7 and 2.8). Figure 2.7 shows positive and negative values concerning variations in annual rainfall in the Sahel region of Africa. Figure 2.8 compares population densities in different parts of a city over a 30 year period.

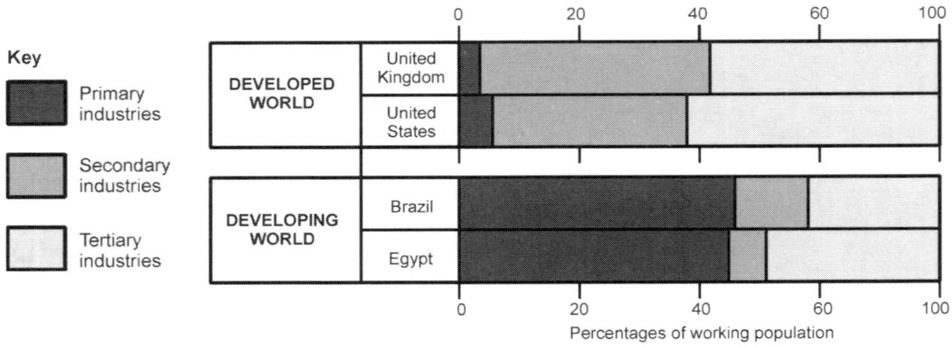

Figure 2.6 Structure of the working population by industry

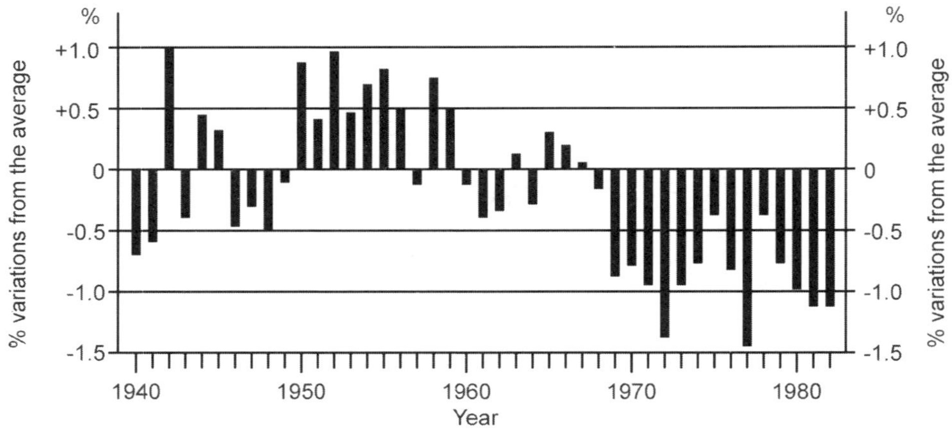

Figure 2.7 Sahel – variations in annual rainfall (1940–1982)

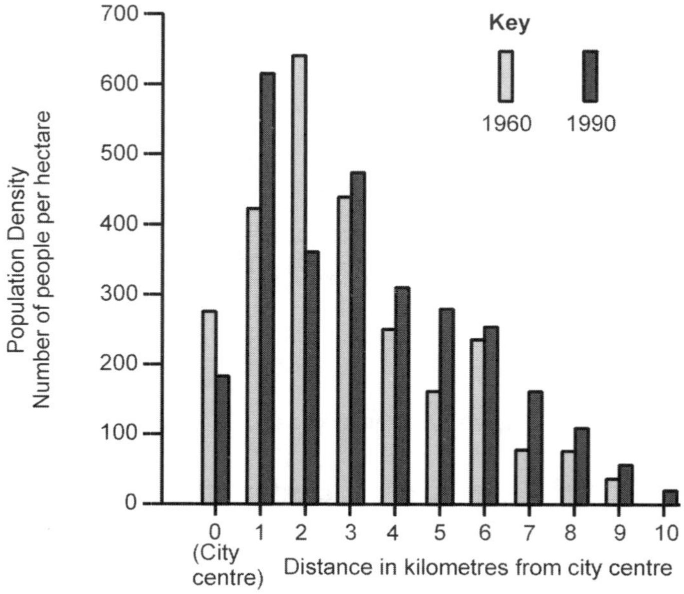

Figure 2.8 Population densities in different parts of a city over a 30 year period

How to read a bar graph

- Look at the heights or lengths of the bars drawn and refer to the vertical or horizontal scale to note the values given to the bars.
- You may notice patterns – for example, which bars are the most important?
- What are the differences between the values of different bars? This may then lead you to ask other questions such as – Why are certain bars more important?

Uses of bar graphs

- To enable comparisons to be made between totals such as monthly rainfall figures.
- To see quickly and easily the contributions to the totals made by parts when divided bar graphs are drawn.

Triangular graphs

- This type of graph has three axes by using the sides of a triangle.
- The shape is an equilateral triangle.
- A triangular graph is used to plot three different sets of data. In the example on page 32 a triangular graph has been drawn to show the employment structure in a number of selected countries.

Stages in the construction of a triangular graph

- Draw an equilateral triangle and divide each side or axis into 10 parts, each to represent 10% – see Figure 2.9.
- The base line scale shows the percentage of the working population employed in primary industries (0–100%) working in the direction of the arrow.
- The right-hand scale shows the percentage employed in secondary industries (0–100%) working in the direction of the arrow.
- The left-hand scale shows the percentage employed in tertiary industries (0–100%) working in the direction of the arrow.
- Points are plotted with reference to the scales on each side or axis of the triangle.

In Figure 2.9 a number of countries have been plotted. I will show you how these were plotted with reference to Japan. Dotted lines have been drawn to explain how the dot for Japan was positioned in the triangle.

The contributions of primary, secondary and tertiary industries in Japan are as follows:

primary industries	13%
secondary industries	39%
tertiary industries	48%

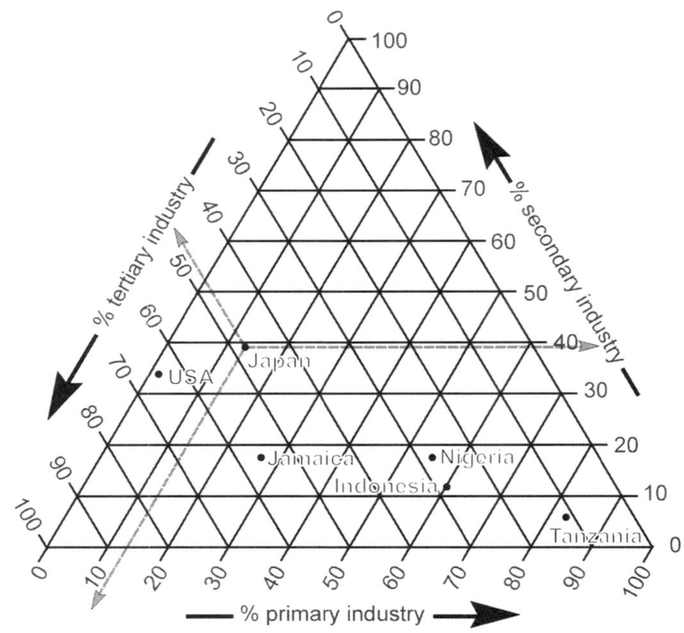

Figure 2.9 Employment structure in a number of selected countries

On Figure 2.9 a dot is located where the dotted line for 13% on the base line scale meets the 39% line on the right hand scale. To check that this location is correct, reference can be made to the left-hand scale. Here the dot is seen to lie on the dotted line showing 48%, which is correct in that all three percentage values add up to 100%.

- Make sure that all three sides of the triangle or axes are clearly labelled and that the scale is clearly stated along each.

How to read a triangular graph

- You can see the relative importance of the three different types of industry, shown in the example on Figure 2.9, by noting the position of the dot within the triangle.
- When you are reading values from a triangular graph make sure that your eye continues to move in the same direction around the sides of the triangle – ANTI-CLOCKWISE in the example shown.
- Look for groupings of dots. In the example given you can see that dots for the developed countries tend to be grouped together because they have similar employment structures. Service and manufacturing industries are much more important than primary industries. In developing countries, primary industries are much more important than the other two sectors of industry.

Glossary
ANTI-CLOCKWISE – movement in the opposite direction as the hands of a clock

Uses of triangular graphs

- They are used when three different types of values are to be compared, for example, three types of industry in the example shown, three uses of buildings along streets in a CBD – offices, specialist shops and convenience shops, etc.

Hint
From the different types of graphs, you can decide which graphical method you would use to represent data.

Note Figure 2.9 portrayed the employment structure of countries on a triangular graph. Figure 2.6 expressed similar information in a divided bar graph. The most important fact to bear in mind is which of the alternatives show the data to best effect. Ease of construction might influence your choice if they both convey the data favourably.

Radial graphs

- These graphs show lines radiating from a central point to represent distances or directions. Figure 2.10 below shows how far people travel from one part of a city for different services. The four main service groups are labelled A, B, C and D.

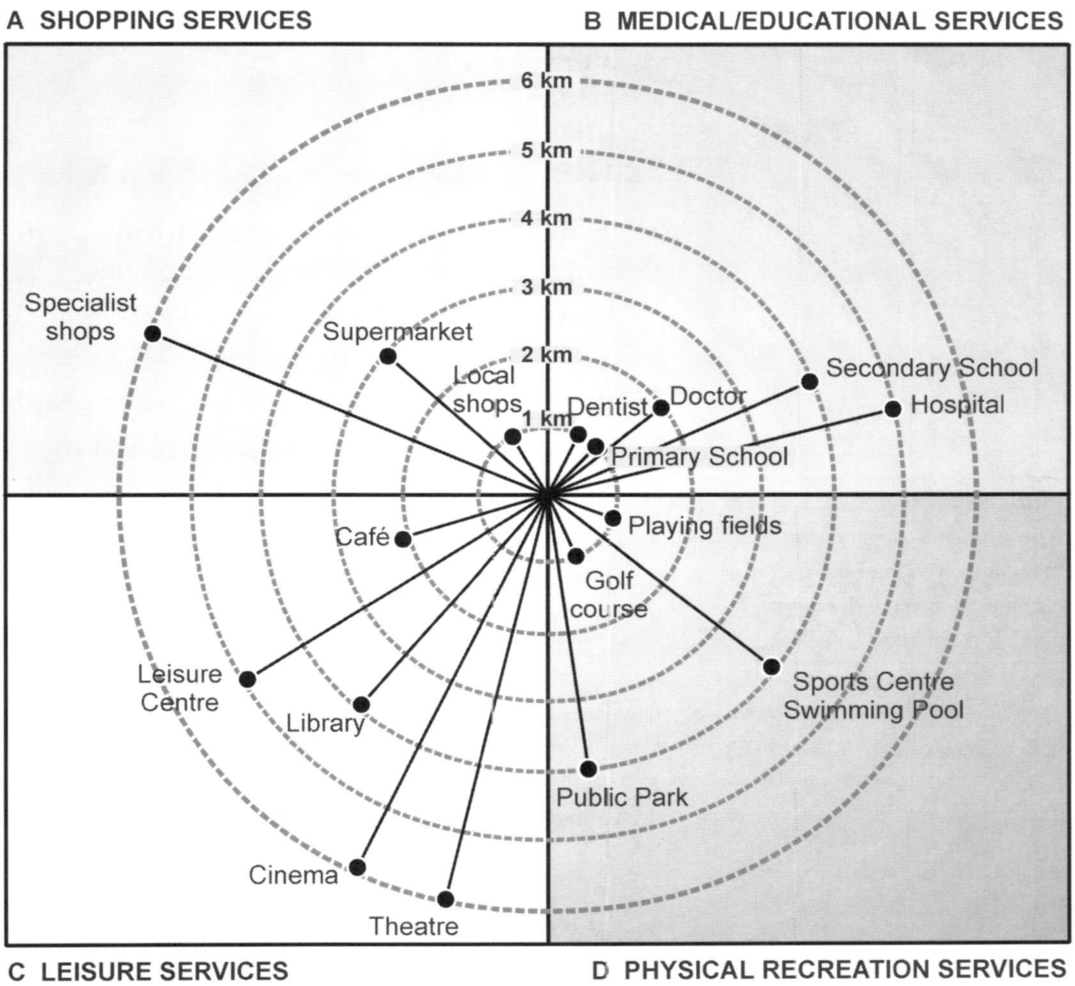

Figure 2.10 Distances people travel from one part of a city for different services

Stages in the construction of a radial graph:

- Select a scale for the lines to be drawn. Bear in mind the values you need to show and the space available on the paper. We have chosen 1 centimetre = 1 kilometre in Figure 2.10.
- Draw concentric circles with a compass to represent distances or numbers. In Figure 2.10 circles represent distances in kilometres. The central point represents the position of the part of the city concerned. Each of the circles has been labelled with a value in kilometres.

- Draw straight lines to scale with a ruler from the central point to represent the distances travelled. Make use of the circles as a guide to the length of each line.

How to read a radial graph

- Look at the lines radiating from the central point to note which are the longest and which the shortest.
- Look for trends – groupings of lines at certain lengths.

Uses of radial graphs

- To give an instant picture of a situation, with good visual impact.
- To allow comparisons to be made if several are drawn side by side or on a map.

Scatter graphs

- On a scatter graph two sets of data are plotted against each other.
- As with a line graph reference is made to two axes, the x axis (horizontal) and the y axis (vertical).

Stages in the construction of a scatter graph

Hint
A best fit line is a line drawn through the centre of the dot distribution to show the general trend, see Figure 2.11a below.

- Choose an appropriate scale for each of the two axes to represent the two sets of data to be shown.
- Plot dots on the graph where certain values on the x axis meet others on the y axis, as can be seen in the example below.
- You may add a **'best fit line'** to the graph when the dots have been plotted.

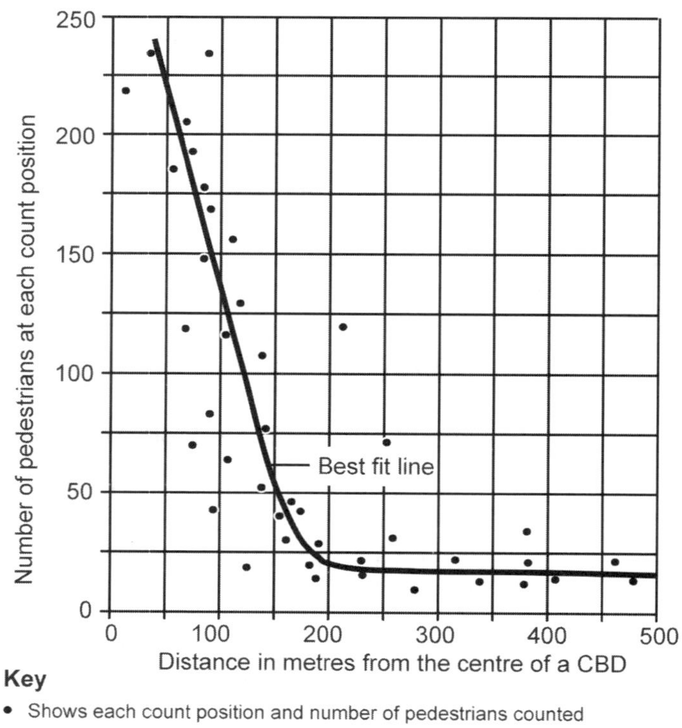

Figure 2.11a Scatter graph to show the results of pedestrian counts in and around a CBD

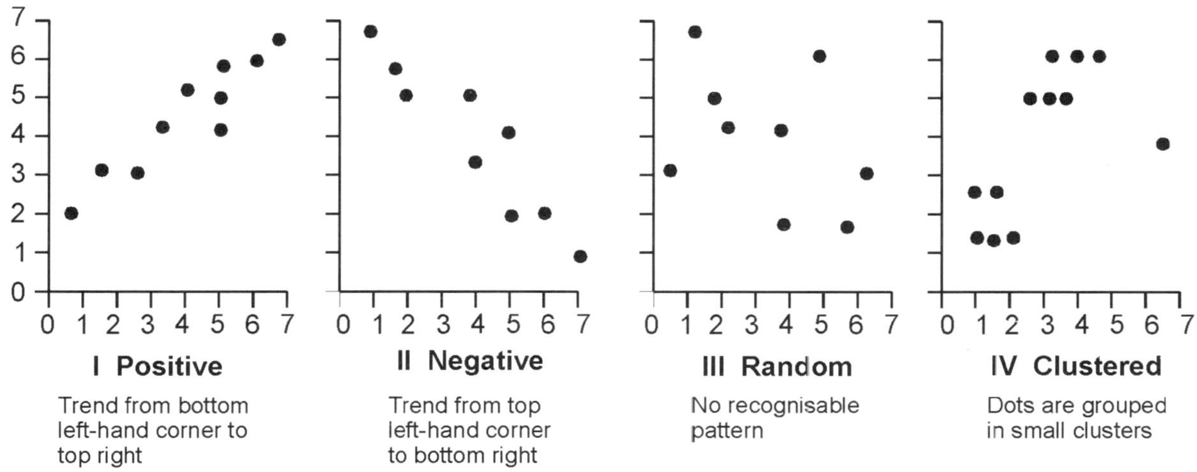

Figure 2.11b Scatter graphs I–IV

How to read a scatter graph

- Look for a pattern shown by the dots on the graph or by the best fit line (if one is drawn). Four main types of pattern may be recognised – see scatter graphs **I–IV** above.

Uses of scatter graphs

- To see whether a relationship exists between two sets of data.

Compound line graphs

Compound line graphs are of two types:

- those showing line graphs for each of the parts as well as the total amount (see Figure 2.12)
- those where each line graph is drawn separately and they overlap (see Figure 2.13).

Stages in the construction of a compound line graph

where each of the parts as well as the total amount is shown (see Figure 2.12)

- Draw a line graph for the first part (usually the largest).
- Use this line as a base line for drawing the line graph for the next part. Other line graphs for the remaining parts are drawn in the same way. Sometimes the space between two neighbouring line graphs is shaded or coloured to highlight the contribution made by each part.

where each line graph is drawn separately and they overlap (see Figure 2.13)

- Draw separate line graphs with reference to the x axis and y axis as explained earlier in the section on drawing line graphs.

How to read a compound line graph as illustrated by Figure 2.12

- Read the total by looking at the uppermost line graph and by referring to the key on the x axis and the y axis.

- Note the contribution made by each part by looking at the spaces shown between two line graphs. Remember these areas may be shaded or coloured.

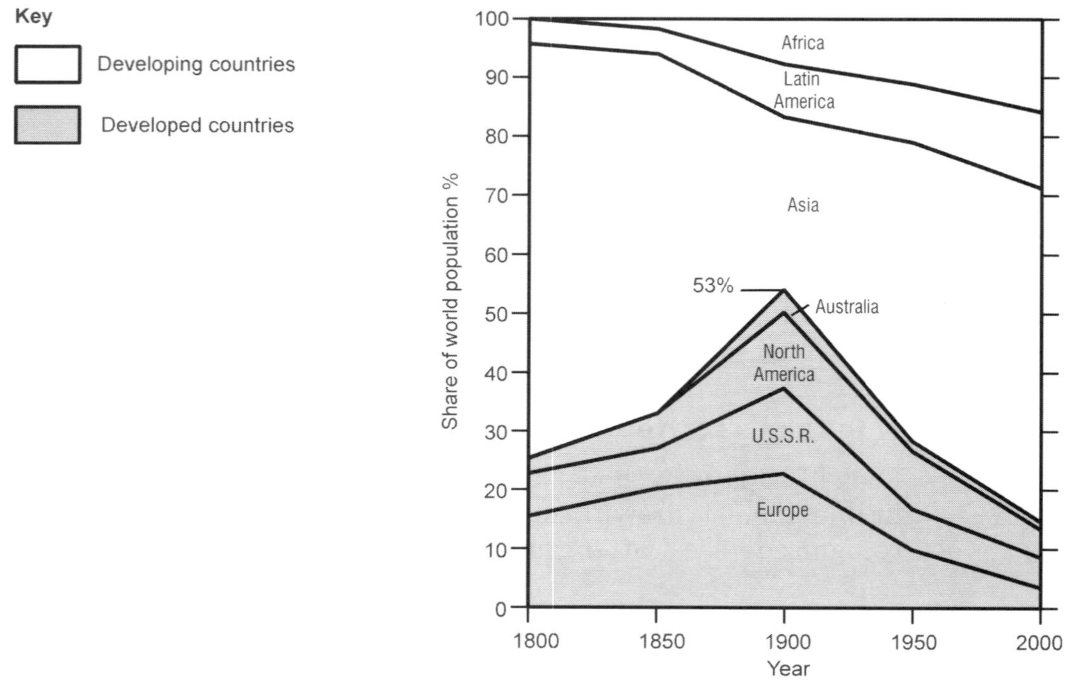

Figure 2.12 The developed and developing countries' share of the world's population, 1800–2000

How to read a compound line graph as illustrated by Figure 2.13

- Read each line graph separately referring to the x axis and the y axis.

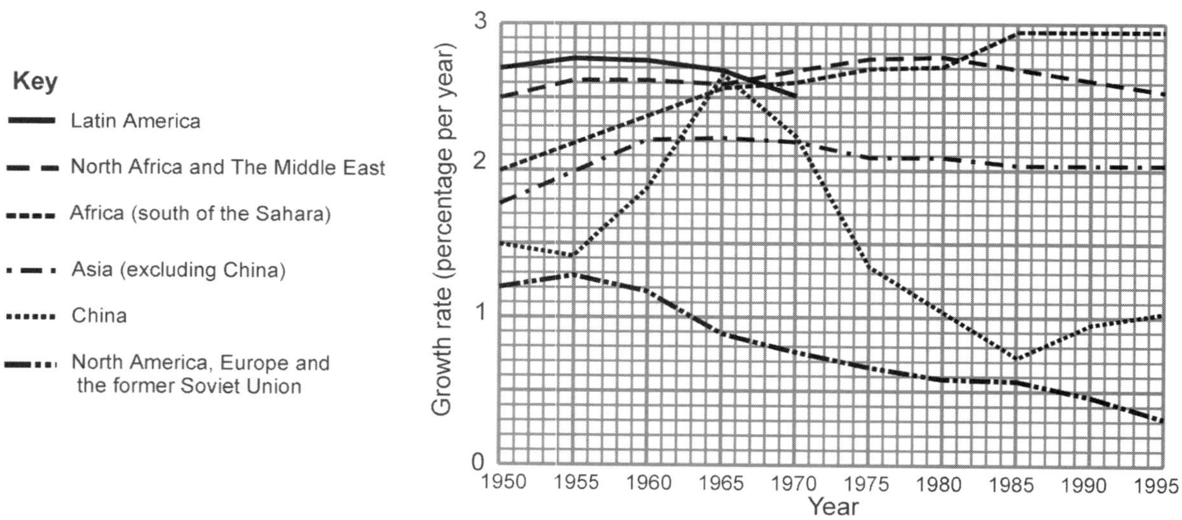

Figure 2.13 Trends in population growth rates 1950 to 1995

Uses of compound line graphs

The type of graph in Figure 2.12 is often used to show how both the total and the contribution of the parts may change. The type of graph in Figure 2.13 is used to compare the contribution of parts only or totals only. Both types are commonly used to show production figures over time.

ACTIVITY 2

Answers are found on page 54.

1 What are the main differences in the structure of the working population in countries of the developed world and countries in the developing world as shown by Figure 2.6 on page 30?

2 What was the main feature of the annual rainfall in the Sahel region of North Africa after 1970 as shown by Figure 2.7 on page 30?

3 Refer to Figure 2.8 on page 30.

State the distance from the city centre with the highest population density in

a 1960

b 1990.

4 From Figure 2.9 on page 32, state the percentage employment in Indonesia in

a primary industries

b secondary industries

c tertiary industries.

5 **a** Look at Figure 2.10 on page 33 and state how far residents in the part of the city shown would travel

i to visit specialist shops

ii to visit the library.

b State and briefly explain why people in this part of the city would travel different distances for the different shopping services shown.

6 Look at the 'best fit line' on Figure 2.11 on page 34 and state which of the following patterns it shows:

A positive

B negative

C random

D clustered.

7 Study Figure 2.12 on page 36.

a State in which year the developed countries had the largest share of the world's population.

b What is their share in 2000?

B Maps

Maps are fundamental to geographers for showing locations and distribution. In this section we will consider a number of different types of maps to see how each is constructed, may be interpreted and for what purposes it may be used.

The types of maps to be reviewed include:

- Dot maps
- Isoline maps

- Choropleth maps
- Sketch maps

Dot maps

Dots may be added to an outline map to show actual locations. It is not always possible for 1 dot to represent 1 unit and so usually a scale has to be used. One problem in choosing a scale may be that dots become so numerous in some parts of the map that they merge. Equally, a difficulty may occur if the scale chosen means that dots are too widely spaced and a pattern is difficult to recognise. It is worth spending some time to determine a correct scale in order that these problems do not occur. On some maps different coloured dots may be used to represent the location of different features, such as types of buildings in an urban area.

Figure 2.14 below shows how dots can be used on an outline map to show the distribution of population in a district. Map A shows the main settled areas within the district. Map B is a dot map showing the numbers of people living in the district. Note how Map A can be used as a guide as to where to place the dots in Map B.

Hint
Dot maps, isoline maps and choropleth maps discussed here are mainly for the benefit of those attempting the HIGCSE examination. They are less significant to those preparing for the IGCSE examination.

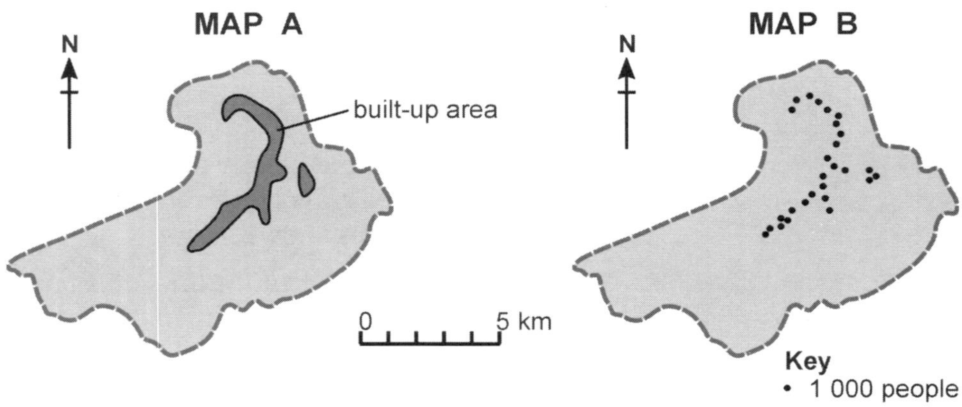

District with built-up area

Dot map showing distribution of population in the district

Figure 2.14

Isoline maps

On these maps lines are drawn to join up points of equal value. In Unit 1 we discussed contour lines as a means of showing heights on topographical maps. Contour lines are examples of isolines in that they join up places of the same height. On weather maps isobars are seen joining up places with equal pressure. These are examples of isolines also.

Figure 2.15 is a partially completed isoline map showing the average number of services provided by Town A which are used by people in surrounding villages. We will refer to this example to illustrate how isoline maps are constructed.

Stages in the construction of an isoline map

- Values are plotted on the map outline as points. On Figure 2.15 these mark the actual positions of villages.
- Decide on the interval you wish to have between the lines. This will depend on the RANGE OF VALUES. It is worth spending some time thinking about this. You do not want too many or too few lines on the map.
- After selecting an interval, you need to draw the lines carefully by joining up points of equal value. To show how this task is undertaken look at Figure 2.15. Here we have decided upon an interval of 3. You will notice that the isoline for the value of 9 has been completed. This was drawn by first of all joining up the points 9 to the east of Town A. To the north of the town we need to continue this line between 6 and 10, nearer to 10, to the west of the town between 3 and 10, nearer to 10, midway between 8 and 10. To the south of the town between 7 and 10, again nearer to 10.

Glossary
RANGE OF VALUES – the difference between the highest and the lowest value

Key
• Villages around Town A
The figures show the average number of services of Town A normally used by people in each village
Isoline for the value of 9

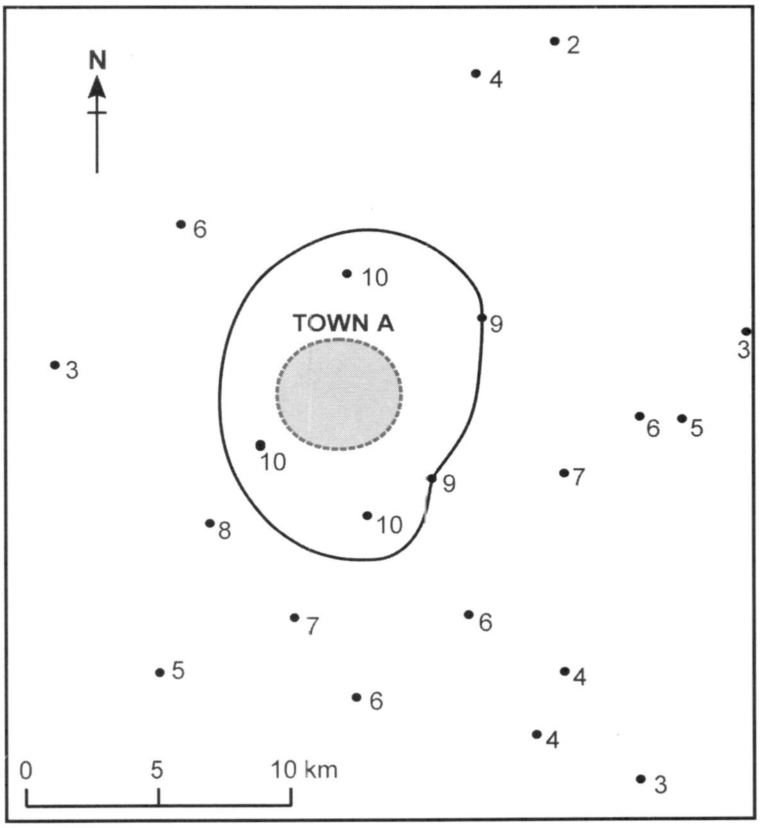

Figure 2.15 Average number of services of town A used by people in surrounding villages

ACTIVITY 3

The answer is on page 55.

Use a pencil to draw in isolines for values of 3 and 6 on Figure 2.15.

Choropleth maps

These maps are used when average data for areas is to be plotted, such as population density, in other words, the number of people in an area.

Stages in the construction of a choropleth map

Glossary
CLASSES – groups
CLASS INTERVALS – range of values within a class

- A map needs to be obtained to show area boundaries, such as the District boundaries in Namibia seen on Figure 2.16.
- Group the data into CLASSES. Do not choose too many otherwise differences will not be obvious on the map. If there are too few classes, differences may not show up either. About 4 to 8 classes would be a reasonable number. The CLASS INTERVAL should be the same throughout. Sometimes this is not always possible and the class intervals may vary. On Figure 2.16, for example, the class intervals are not constant.
- Select shading or shades of colours for the classes. Grade your shading so that the closest or densest shading is used for the classes you wish to emphasise, usually the highest values.
- Add shading to the base map which has on it the area boundaries.
- Provide a key and a title to the map.

Figure 2.16 below shows population density in the Districts of Namibia.

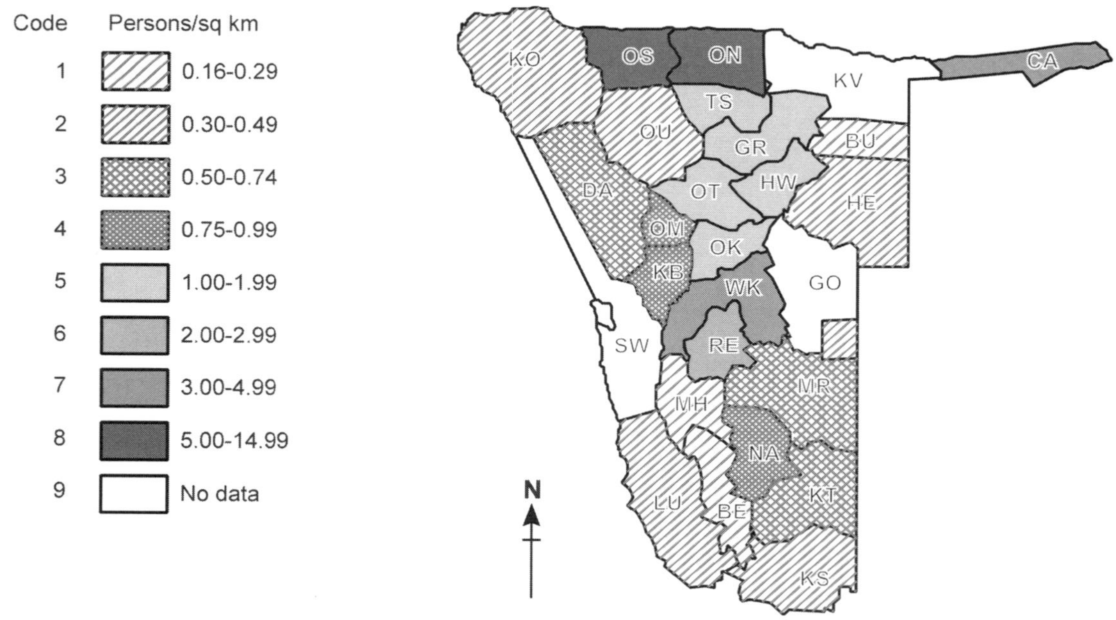

Figure 2.16 Population density (Namibia) by Districts – 1991

ACTIVITY 4

Answers are on page 55.

1 Calculate the population density of the Gobabis District.

District	Population (1991)	Area (sq.km.)	Population density
Swakopmund (SW)	20 750	44 700	0.46
Kavango (KV)	136 600	45 700	2.99
Gobabis (GO)	28 000	46 000	?

2 Referring to the key to the map, state the code number of the shading you would use to show the population density in each of:

a Swakopmund **b** Kavango **c** Gobabis.

Sketch maps

These are invaluable to a geographer in summarising information. They may include references to locations, distribution of features and reasoning.

In the examination, a sketch map may save you time in answering a question. You can often draw a sketch map more quickly than writing out an answer. Do not repeat information with a written account when you have already provided this detail on a sketch map. You only receive credit once in the answer, however you present information. Sometimes you are asked to draw sketch maps from a topographical map. In this case the question would specify what to include. You may be required to show the main physical regions or features of the drainage for example. In both of these you should only include on your sketch map the features asked for and not be tempted to include information on farming, settlement or other aspects of human geography shown on the topographical map.

Sketch maps have a valuable role to play in coursework assignments. Here, however, they should be more accurate than those drawn from memory in an examination paper. Sketch maps are sometimes included in examination questions for you to analyse and use in relation to the question set. Look at the sketch map (Figure 2.19) given for example with a photograph in Section D, page 45. This was a question included on IGCSE Paper 3, the practical paper, and details on the sketch map were to be related to the photograph.

Hint
In both the IGCSE and HIGCSE examinations an instruction on the front of the examination papers states that 'sketch maps and diagrams should be drawn whenever they serve to illustrate an answer'.
Sketch maps lack the precision associated with the maps already discussed in this section.

C Diagrams

In addition to the various types of maps discussed in the previous section, geographers make use of a wide range of diagrams. These include those drawn with close attention to accuracy, such as population pyramids, to others such as sketch diagrams which present details in a less accurate form. Diagrams are meant to be informative and at times can present ideas more effectively than by the written word.

Geographers use so many different types of diagrams that only a selection can be considered here. It will pay dividends if you familiarise yourself with different types of diagrams used throughout the four modules.

Three main types of diagram will now be described to show their uses and importance in the study of geography:

- population pyramids
- models
- explanatory diagrams.

Population pyramids

This form of diagram deserves particular attention because of its importance in understanding a number of significant features about people living in an area. The two main aspects of population shown by a population pyramid are:

- the number of people in each age group
- the proportion of males and females in the population.

A number of population pyramids are shown in Section C of Unit 1 in Module 1. You can see by looking at one of these population pyramids that the **vertical** scale provides details of the age groups in the population. The youngest age group is always shown at the base and the oldest at the top of the pyramid. Usually the age groups are given in blocks of years; 0–4 years, 5–9 years etc. The **horizontal** scale informs you of the percentage or total in each age group. Details concerning males of the population are always given on the left-hand side of the population pyramid, female details are on the right-hand side.

To obtain the maximum use from a population pyramid, refer to those in Section C of Unit 1 in Module 1 and consider the following points:

- Note the area named in the title and the date to which it relates.
- Look at its **general shape**. A broad base indicates a large percentage or number in the 'young' age groups. A marked narrowing of the population pyramid tells us that there are relatively few in the upper age groups. A balanced pyramid is shown by an even shape.
- Note the **percentage** or **number of people** in the three major groups of the population pyramid 0–14 years, 15–60 years and over 60 years. The 0–14 years and over 60 years form the dependent population groups who rely upon the working age group 15–60 years.
- Study the **balance** between the **males and females** in the population. This is known as the sex ratio. Some population pyramids may show large numbers in the working age groups, especially the younger of these groups. There may also be more males than females in these groups. This situation would suggest that immigration is an important feature of this population. It is young adults, mostly males, who form the dominant element in migration.

Population pyramids provide a great deal of information on a number of aspects of population study, including the relationship between different sectors – young / old, male / female, dependent / independent sectors. In addition they indicate important trends in birth rate and life expectancy. By studying those for different countries or regions, or for the same place over different time periods, useful comparisons may be made.

Models

Models summarise ideas which may be tested against a real situation. They are used to simplify explanations. Figure 2.17 below shows a model which may be used to present ideas on the location of different regions which may develop in a city in a developing country. It may be compared with a map showing the urban regions of an actual city you know to see what similarities and differences there are. You may then suggest reasons as to whether the model is useful or not in explaining the LAYOUT of these urban regions. Simple models, such as Figure 2.17, are sometimes given in examination questions for you to describe or to explain.

Glossary
LAYOUT – arrangement or plan

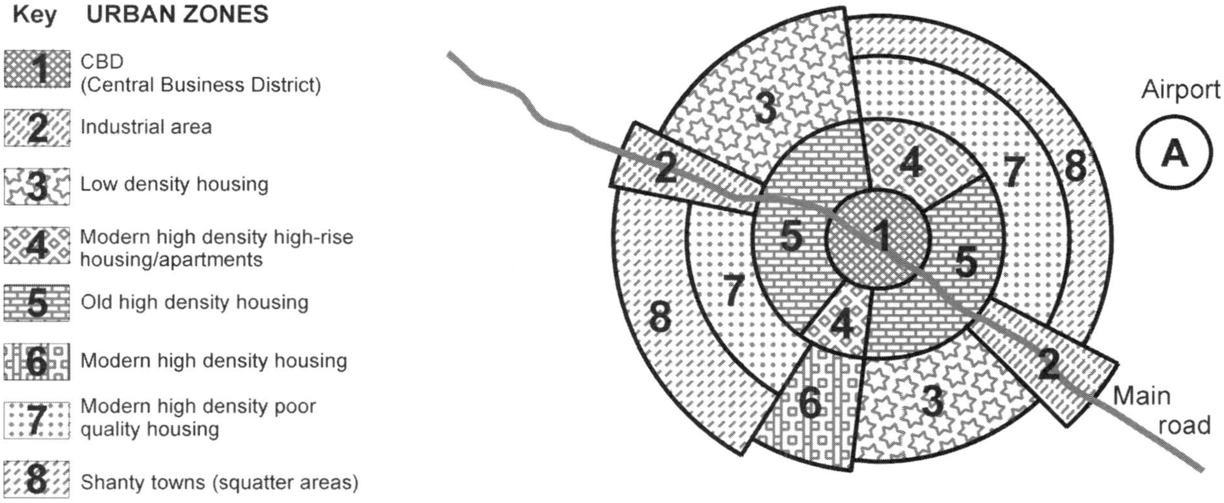

Figure 2.17 Model of land use in a city in a developing country

Explanatory diagrams

These are diagrams which are used to describe and explain features. By glancing at Module 2, a number of different diagrams may be seen which are of this type, for example, those showing landforms and weather instruments. These diagrams save lengthy written explanations and they also show you what the feature looks like, its shape, size and main characteristics.

It is important to realise that the value of these diagrams depends upon the quality of the ANNOTATIONS attached to the drawing. In the examination you will be encouraged to include diagrams of this type as part of your answer. Like sketch maps, described in Section B, they provide you with an alternative way of presenting information and they may save you time in an examination. Diagrams sometimes feature as part of questions for you to label, describe and explain what is shown.

> **Glossary**
> ANNOTATIONS – notes or labels

One special kind of explanatory diagram is when notes are linked by lines or arrows. These are sometimes called flow diagrams. Figure 2.18 shows reasons why farmers in many parts of the developing world are caught in a poverty trap. By following the arrows we see how such a situation may arise.

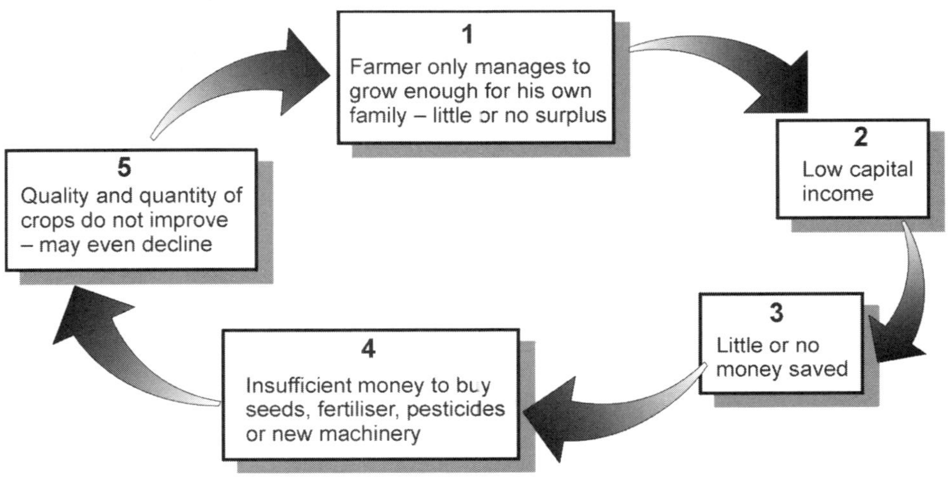

Figure 2.18 Diagram to show problems faced by many subsistence farmers in developing countries

D Photographic and pictorial material

Photographs

Photographs add realism to the study of Geography. Ideally the subject should be studied away from the classroom using real situations, as in fieldwork. This is not always possible and one way in which we can make Geography more of a living subject is to use representations of reality such as photographs.

In examinations, photographs test the ability of a learner

- to recognise features
- to recognise patterns and relationships.

Points to bear in mind when looking at photographs relate to the type of photograph presented to you.

- **a vertical aerial photograph** will have been taken vertically over a landscape. This type of photograph is like a large-scale map of an area. It is more difficult to interpret than a map because it lacks helpful symbols and other information which help you to identify features.
- **an oblique aerial photograph** shows a landscape from an oblique angle, not vertically. The photograph on page 45 is an example of this type of photograph showing a spit in a river estuary.
- **a photograph taken from a position on the ground** may include an extensive area if it was taken from a high elevation. On the other hand it may be a close-up such as a landscape feature, vegetation, a building, etc.

Hint
Look at the photograph in Activity 7, Unit 1 of this module.

Glossary
FOREGROUND – the area in the front of the photograph
BACKGROUND – the area in the rear of the photograph

When looking at a photograph for the first time, try to take in the picture as a whole to set the scene. Then consider the details which make up the photograph. Photographs are not always selective in what they show. In aerial photographs *all* features of the landscape are shown. Some of these may be irrelevant for the purpose that you wish to use the photograph. Try to be selective when you study a photograph. Use the terms 'FOREGROUND' and 'BACKGROUND' if the photograph shows an extensive area.

Sometimes an aerial photograph may be presented in an examination along with a large-scale map or a sketch map of the area shown on the photograph. The question set usually tests your skill in relating places shown on the photograph to map details. You need to translate photographic details by using map information.

Examples of map information which may be useful when interpreting photographs are **distances** and **directions**. Both of these can be calculated from the map and applied to a description of the photograph. A common question requires you to give the direction in which the camera was pointing when the photograph was taken.

To do this effectively, line up features shown on the photograph with the corresponding features on the map, then refer to the **directional arrow** shown on the map in order to answer the question. On occasions certain features shown on a photograph are not evidenced on the map or vice versa. This provides useful evidence if you need to determine which was completed first, the map or the photograph.

When you are interpreting a photograph make sure that what you describe is what you see. Sometimes it can be useful to draw sketches or diagrams to help you to interpret photographs. Practice by interpreting the photographs in the four modules and ones you may see in other books, magazines and newspapers.

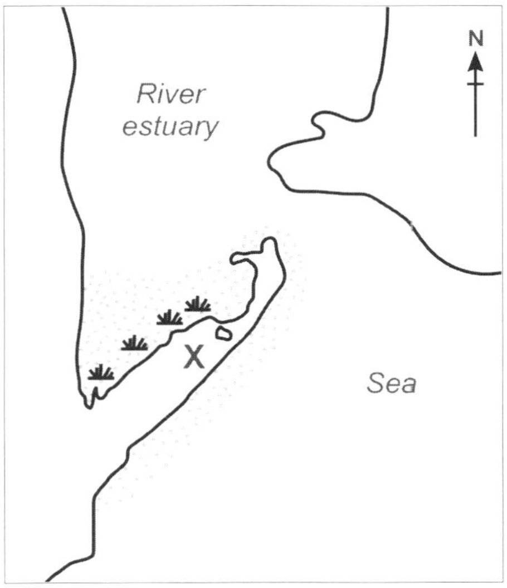

Hint
You will use this sketch map and photograph later in this unit.

Figure 2.19 A sketch map and a corresponding photograph

Field sketches

Hint
When drawing field sketches, you should have a rubber with you for any alterations that you want to make.

These are sketch diagrams that are drawn when doing field work as part of coursework. A field sketch is only one option in recording information when you are out-of-doors doing an investigation. A photograph is more accurate but with a field sketch you can be selective and emphasise points which are of particular interest. Rough sketches can be made in the field. When drawing sketches in the field remember the following points.

- Sketch diagrams should be drawn in pencil
- Draw bold outlines.
- Do not include too much detail in your drawings. Simple annotated sketches are the most useful.
- Add details such as the location of the sketch and the direction you were facing when the sketch was made.
- Neat sketches based upon the rough drafts produced outside can be drawn later, when you write up your assignment.

Figure 2.20 overleaf is a neat field sketch produced by a learner which shows details of a footpath as part of a study to show the characteristics and development of footpaths in a coastal area.

The schist fragments on the path have an average length of 10 cm. With this size they have not been removed by concentrated water action. The clay matrix has largely been washed away. Erosion in the centre of the path has been aided by loosening and disturbance by people walking along the path to the beach.

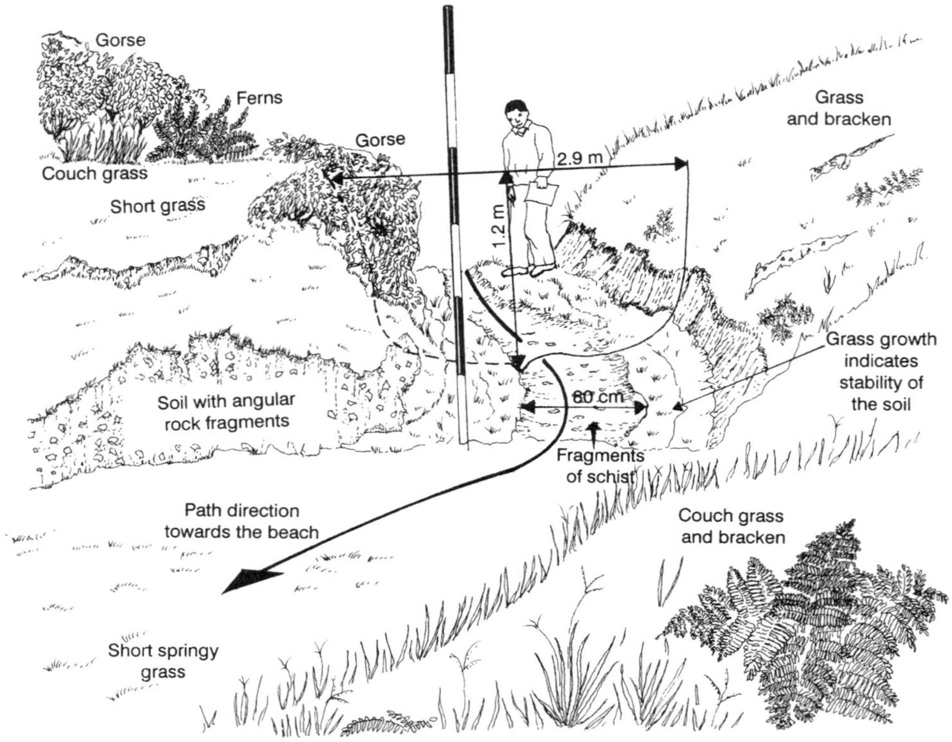

Figure 2.20 A field sketch showing details of a footpath in a coastal area

Other pictorial techniques

Examiners sometimes test your skill at interpreting and analysing information by presenting it in pictorial form, such as in the form of a **cartoon**. The aim is to present you with a labelled drawing or drawings from which you should come up with some ideas.

Figure 2.21 below appeared in a HIGCSE geography examination. Candidates were invited to use the ideas in the cartoon to suggest how aid given by developed countries to developing countries may bring further problems as well as advantages.

Figure 2.21 A cartoon showing how aid may bring problems

ACTIVITY 5

Answers are on page 55.

What messages is the cartoon (Figure 2.21) trying to get across?

E Tables of data

As you have seen in Modules 1, 2 and 3, statistics play an important part in all aspects of the subject. Data or statistics on population, climate and meteorology as well as economic activities are fundamental to our understanding in geography. You should be able to describe, analyse and recognise trends in data provided. You should also be able to suggest an appropriate way of presenting data in graphs and maps. We have already given you advice on this in Sections A and B of this Unit. Here you are going to look at ways of describing and analysing features and trends from statistics presented to you.

It is easy to be bewildered by data when you first look at it. In order to make the most of the data, you need to have a plan of action.

- Firstly **familiarise** yourself with the data. Look carefully to see what sort of data it is – actual numbers or percentages. Note the title given to the table and headings given to the columns of data.
- Begin to sort out the **statistics**. What are the highest and lowest values?
- See if there is a **general pattern or trend**. Do not concern yourself yet with details. Always work from the general to specific details.
- Look later to see if there are **exceptions** to the general pattern or trend.

You can apply this plan of action to the table of data below that shows climatic details for Cape Town in South Africa.

Temperature – average monthly °C											
J	F	M	A	M	J	J	A	S	O	N	D
21	20	20	17	14	13	12	12	14	16	18	20

Rainfall – monthly totals mm											
J	F	M	A	M	J	J	A	S	O	N	D
12	19	17	42	67	98	68	76	36	45	12	13

Annual Total 505 mm

You can see from looking at this data that temperatures are highest at the beginning and end of the year (the southern hemisphere summer). Rainfall is lowest at this time of the year.

The maximum monthly temperature is 21 °C in January, the lowest monthly temperature is 12 °C in July and August. The annual temperature range is therefore 9 °C.

The rainfall figures show that summer is the dry season with only 73 mm from November to March. Most of the annual rainfall occurs in winter with a total of 432 mm from April to October.

Now looking for exceptions, you can see that while the rainfall declines from August (76 mm) to 36 mm in September, it rises again in October before falling in the summer months (November to March). The pattern we have described is characteristic of a Mediterranean climate which you studied in Module 2.

ACTIVITY 6

Answers are on pages 55 and 56.

The data shown in Table 2 can be used to measure the quality of life of people in a number of countries.

Table 2

country	GNP (US $) (per capita)	birth rate (per 1 000)	death rate (per 1 000)	life expectancy (years)	population per doctor	literacy (%)
Ethiopia	100	48	18	47	33 000	33
India	300	31	10	60	2 500	50
Nigeria	320	47	14	53	6 000	53
Namibia	1 700	42	11	59	4 600	40
South Africa	3 000	31	9	63	1 750	81
Saudi Arabia	8 000	42	7	66	700	61
Australia	18 000	14	8	77	230	99
USA	25 000	14	9	76	420	99

Hint
To make it easier to use this data, countries are listed according to their GNP, starting with the country with the lowest GNP value.

Glossary
GNP – Gross National Product
GNP PER CAPITA – value of GNP divided by total population
GROWTH RATE – birth rate minus death rate

1 What general relationships exist between GNP PER CAPITA and

a GROWTH RATE of population **b** life expectancy

c medical facilities **d** literacy?

2 For each of 1a, b, c and d, name **one** country which is especially out of line with the general relationship you have described in Question 1.

3 Briefly explain why the country you have named in each of 2 a, b, c and d is out of line.

To give more precise answers to Questions 1–4 above, a series of scatter graphs could be drawn. However, from studying the data in Table 2, using your plan of action, you can deduce some useful relationships. In your study of Geography, evidence from analysing data can lead you to investigate further ideas. It may be necessary to process data presented to you in order to make the most effective use of it. Simple calculations allow you to refine raw data which may enable you to see patterns and trends more clearly.

Hint
Data refinement discussed below is mainly for the benefit of those attempting the HIGCSE examination. It is less important to those preparing for the IGCSE examination.

Three ways of refining data

- The **mean** is the arithmetic average of the values given in the data. It is useful and easy to calculate. On their own, a list of values or figures may not convey much to you, for example, a list of the sizes of pebbles chosen at random on part of a beach, or the production of crops over successive months. A mean may provide a useful guide when making comparisons. To find the mean, add up each of the figures in a data set and divide that total by the number of figures in the data set.

To find the mean monthly temperature of Cape Town from the data given on page 47, add up the monthly temperatures given = 197. Divide this total by 12 (number of months) = 16.4 or 16 °C to the nearest whole figure.

- The **median** is the middle value in a data set. To find the median – list the values or figures in a data set in rank order starting with the highest. Count the number of figures in the data set then add 1 and divide by 2. This gives the middle figure or the position between two figures in the middle. There must be the same number of figures above and below the median.

You can rank the monthly temperatures in °C for Cape Town starting with the highest.

21
20
20
20
18
17
16
14
14
13
12
12

You can see that the median must lie between the sixth and seventh figure listed so that there are six figures above and six figures below. This gives a median value midway between 16 and 17 or 16.5 °C.

The spread of data shown by the list above is sometimes known as the **range**. You can see from the range how the figures in your data set vary. Sometimes you may wish to exclude extreme figures – some of those at the top or bottom of the range because they are not typical and are distorting the range by extending it. To exclude these we can find what is called the **inter-quartile range**. You have already seen how to calculate the median. This divided the data set into half. If you find the middle figure of each half you now have four quarters or **quartiles**. The two in the middle give you the **inter-quartile range**.

- The **mode** is the value which occurs most frequently in a data set. Looking at the monthly temperatures for Cape Town listed above you can see that 20 °C is the mode in that it occurs three times in the list.

Hint
There may be more than one mode if two or more values occur most frequently in a data set.

Of these three ways of refining data – finding the mean, median and mode, the most useful is calculating the mean.

F Written accounts

Geography is about the real world and accounts of actual happenings may provide you with information which may not be available in textbooks. Newspapers, for example, often give you first hand accounts of a recent earthquake, cyclone or other natural hazard. You can learn a great deal about their nature and effects on people by studying these. Look out for this type of newspaper article and extract information from them.

Written accounts, such as newspaper extracts, are sometimes included in examination questions. You will be asked questions on the details provided and you need to be able to separate the relevant details from other information. Look at Unit 1 in Module 2 where an account of the Turkish earthquake in 1999 is given for you, on page 4. There you can see questions based on the newspaper extract.

Summary

The key skills you have learned in this unit relate to the presentation of data in a variety of forms. Geographers are concerned with interpreting graphs, maps, diagrams, photographic and pictorial presentations, tables of data and written accounts. The ability to see patterns and trends from such information is important in your study of geography.

A There are a number of different types of graphs. Each is drawn for a different purpose. In this first section the most important types of graphs were described with the help of examples. You must be able to draw, read and know the purpose of each type of graph described.

B In addition to large-scale topographical maps discussed in Unit 1, you need to become familiar with other types of maps. As with graphs, you have to decide which type of map to use and how it is constructed. You should be able to read details from different types of maps.

C Many different kinds of diagrams are used to show geographical details. As you work through the four modules you will become aware of the variety of diagrams that may be drawn. The examinations encourage you to provide relevant information on diagrams. Questions often contain diagrams for you to describe and analyse.

D Photographs and other pictorial techniques also have much to offer you in your study of geography. These help to bring reality to the subject.

E Tables of data help provide useful details in your study of various topics described in the modules.

F The ability to extract information from written accounts, such as magazine and newspaper articles and the Internet, is important. This adds to the knowledge you gain from the modules. This will make your subject relate to real life and help you to keep up-to-date.

Check your progress

1 Study Figure 2.1 on page 26 and answer the following:

To the nearest billion, state

a the expected growth in world population from 1800 to 2100 [1]

b the expected difference in the population of the Developing Regions and the Developed Regions of the world in 2000. [1]

2 What does Figure 2.2 on page 27 tell you about the numbers of people in the world affected by natural hazards from 1970? [2]

3 Study Figure 2.22 below that shows a series of pie graphs and a table. These show the employment structure in five selected countries. Match the country names given in the table with the numbers of the pie graphs (1–5). [5]

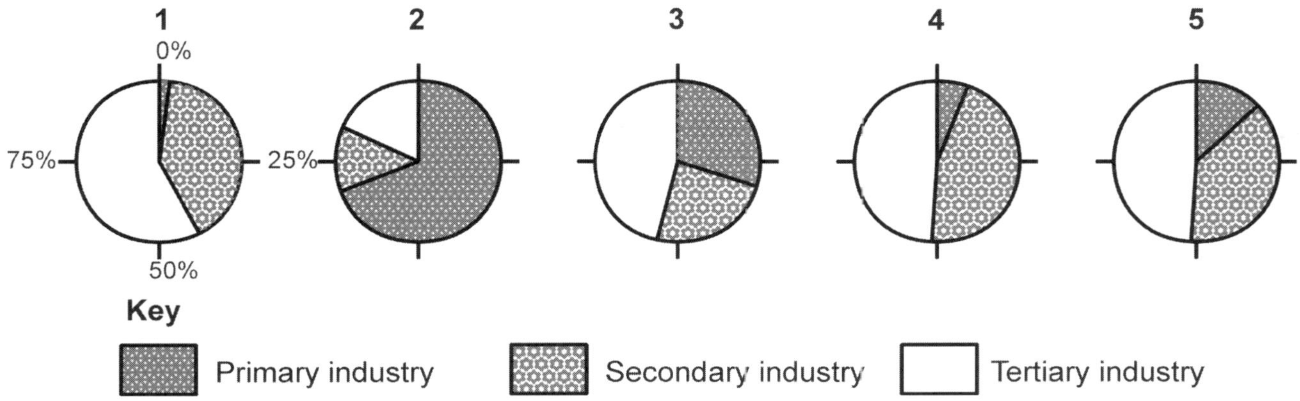

COUNTRY	PERCENTAGE OF WORKERS IN		
	Primary Industry	Secondary Industry	Tertiary Industry
India	69	13	18
Brazil	30	24	46
Japan	13	38	49
The Netherlands	6	45	49
United Kingdom	2	42	56

Figure 2.22

4 From Figure 2.5 on page 29:

a State the two most common natural hazards which occurred in the year shown. [2]

b How many of each were experienced during the year? [2]

5 Refer to the scattergraph (Figure 2.11a on page 34).

a At what distances from the centre of the CBD were the two count positions with the greatest differences from the 'Best Fit Line'? [2]

b How many pedestrians were recorded at each of these two count positions? [2]

6 Study Figure 2.13 on page 36.

a Complete the line for Latin America using the following data:

Percentage growth per year

1975 – 2.3%

1985 – 2.3%

1995 – 1.8% [3]

b What was the population growth rate in Africa (south of the Sahara) in 1950? [1]

c When was the population growth rate in China at its greatest? [1]

d Describe the trend in the population growth rate for North America, Europe and the former Soviet Union. [4]

e By what percentage did the population growth rate change for China from 1950 to 1995? [1]

7 Study the photograph together with Figure 2.19 on page 45.

> **Hint**
> To help you to answer this question see Unit 4 of Module 2 (The Natural Environment)

a In which direction was the camera pointing when the photograph was taken? [1]

b What is the coastal feature labelled X? [1]

c Describe the main characteristics of feature X and the river estuary shown on the photograph. [6]

8 Figure 2.23 below gives information about car production and export by world regions in 1964 and 1990.

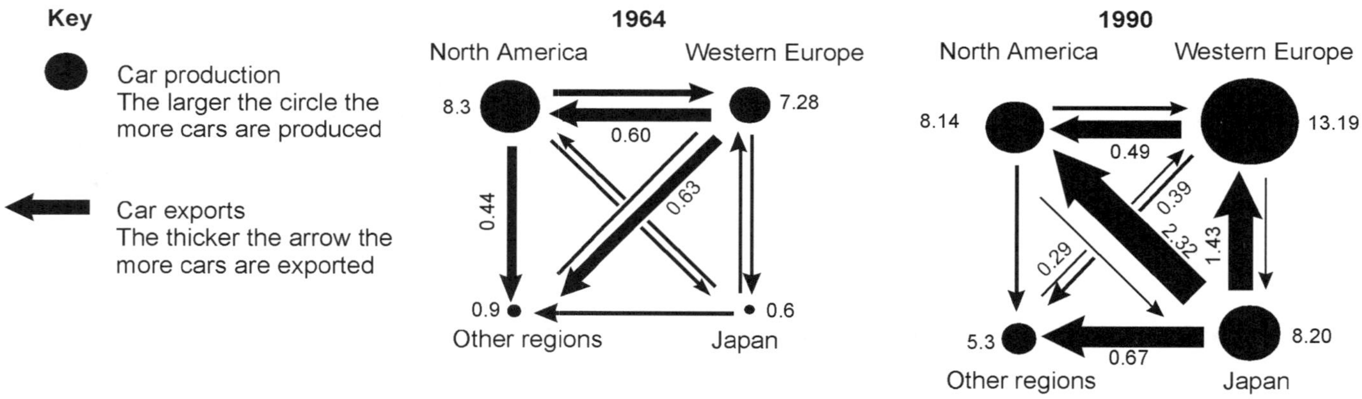

All figures are in million cars. Unlabelled lines show exports less than 0.1 million cars

Figure 2.23 Motor car production and exports by world regions in 1964 and 1990

a What was the increase in the number of cars produced in Western Europe from 1964 to 1990? [1]

b How many cars were exported from Japan in 1990? [1]

c State **three** of the main changes from 1964 to 1990 in each of

i car production [3]

ii car exports [3]

9 Look at Figure 2.24 below which shows the results of a survey of shoppers visiting shops in the centre of a town.

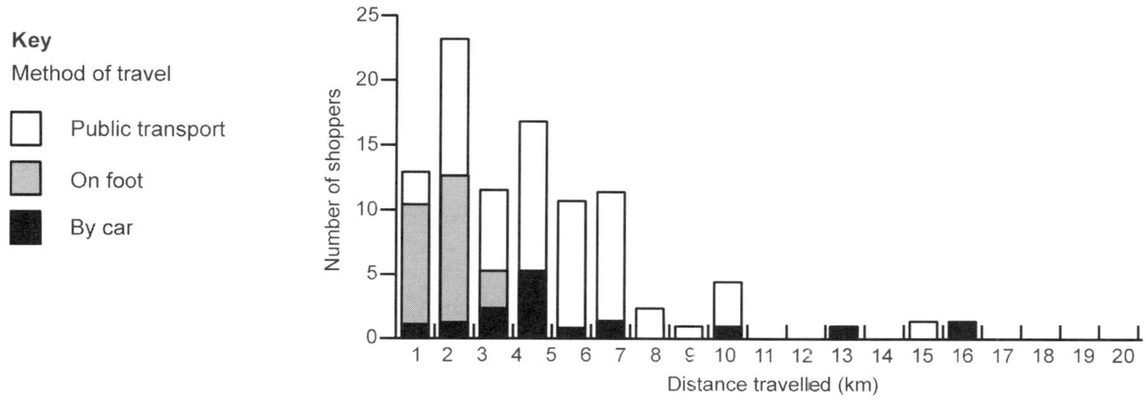

Figure 2.24 The results of a survey of shoppers visiting shops in the centre of a town

a How far from the centre of the town do shoppers

i visit the town

ii travel on foot? [2]

b From which distance from the centre of town

i do most shoppers travel

ii do most shoppers travel by car? [2]

c State three important features shown about travel by public transport. [3]

10 Figure 2.25 below shows water consumption in the United States, the United Kingdom and a number of African countries.

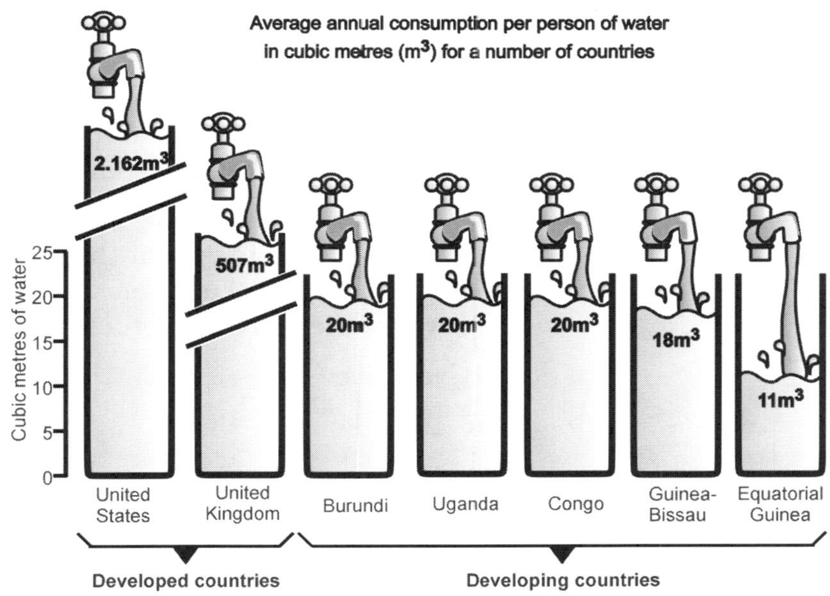

Figure 2.25 World water consumption

a What does the diagram show about the consumption of water? [2]

b What problem faced the artist when this diagram was constructed? [2]

c How was this problem overcome? [2]

Feedback to activities

FEEDBACK 1

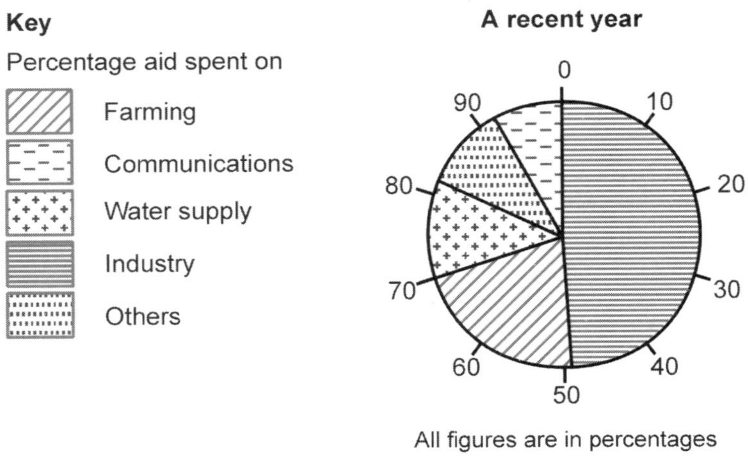

Figure 2.26

FEEDBACK 2

1 Countries in the developed world have a lower percentage of the working population in primary industries and more in both secondary and tertiary industries.

2 Lower than average annual rainfall.

3 **a** 2 km

b 1 km

4 **a** 60%

b 12%

c 28%

5 **a** **i** 6 km

ii 4 km

b People travel further to specialist shops (6 km), 3 km to visit the supermarket and 1 km to visit the local shops.

People visit local shops more frequently to buy everyday goods such as food. They visit the supermarket less often and are willing to travel a larger distance to visit a specialist shop where they buy high order / specialist goods.

6 B Negative

7 **a** 1900

b 15%

FEEDBACK 3

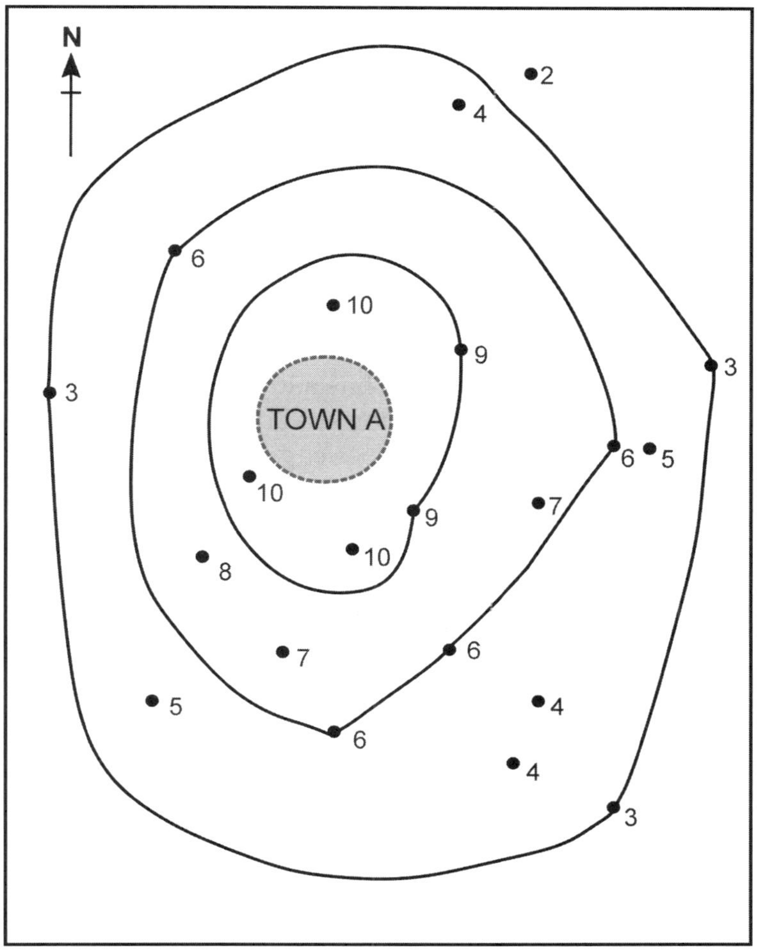

Figure 2.27

FEEDBACK 4

1 $\frac{28\,000}{46\,000} = 0.6$

2 **a** Swakopmund – code 2.

b Kavango – code 6.

c Gobabis – code 3, population density 0.61.

FEEDBACK 5

Aid from more developed countries is welcomed by developing countries but it involves them paying the money back with interest. The more developed countries are trying to influence how the developing countries spend the aid. They wish them to spend over half of the aid in buying goods from the more developed countries.
Is the aid sufficient?

FEEDBACK 6

1 The higher the GNP

a the lower the growth rate of population.

b the greater the life expectancy.

c the smaller the number of people to a doctor.

d the higher the percentage of literate people.

2 **a** Saudi Arabia.

b India.

c India.

d Two answers – Namibia or Saudi Arabia.

3 **a** Saudi Arabia has high GNP per capita but also a high population growth rate.

b India has a higher life expectancy than Nigeria and Namibia and yet has a lower GNP per capita.

c India has a low GNP per capita but also a lower number of people per doctor than both Nigeria and Namibia with a higher GNP per capita.

d Namibia has a lower literacy rate than India and Nigeria and yet has a higher GNP per capita.

Saudi Arabia has a lower literacy rate than South Africa and yet has a higher GNP per capita.

Unit 3
Enquiry skills

When you have completed your study of HIGCSE / IGCSE Geography, you will have developed a number of skills which will serve you well. A group of these skills come together when you undertake any kind of geographical investigation and they are known collectively as geographical enquiry skills.

This means that you will consider a topic or an issue on a local scale that you can investigate first hand by carrying out fieldwork, and then back up your enquiry by secondary information which you can obtain from maps, photographs, documents of various kinds, (for example, newspapers and tables of statistics), films and videos.

Obviously your circumstances as a learner will limit you to what you can achieve. In a face-to-face tuition situation you can carry out the three or four investigations needed to complete coursework which counts towards your final exam mark. If you are learning through distance education, with tutorial support, you will need to understand the steps and the processes of geographical enquiry. You will be examined on your understanding of how to carry out such an enquiry and how to analyse information and present your findings in the alternative to coursework written paper. You may also opt to offer the alternative to coursework paper in a face-to-face learning situation.

This unit is divided into the following sections:

A	Using enquiry skills
B	Choosing a geographical topic
C	Collecting the data
D	Presenting and processing the data
E	Writing a geographical enquiry and analysing data

In this unit you will learn:

- how to conduct geographical enquiries
- how to use suitable geographical techniques (tools) of investigation
- what kinds of information to obtain in support of your enquiries
- how to analyse information
- how to make appropriate judgements and reach conclusions
- how to present the results of geographical enquiries.

To help you understand these steps, firstly, we will consider the coursework exam option and then how to apply enquiry skills to other situations described in the alternative to coursework written paper.

A Using enquiry skills

Undertaking a geographical enquiry can be seen as a process with four parts to it.

1 Choosing a geographical topic.

2 Collecting the data.

3 Presenting and processing the data collected.

4 Writing about and analysing the data collected.

The different stages in a full enquiry process based upon fieldwork can be shown in more detail by the use of a flow chart, shown in Table 1.

Table 1 Flow chart for the enquiry process.

Geographical topic identified and chosen

↓

Title agreed and study aims worked out and stated

↓

Primary data collected by fieldwork using one or more of the following ways; questionnaires; observation; counts; measurement

↓

Other written sources of data consulted and used

↓

Data collected is organised and recorded, for example in tables and tally charts

↓

Data is processed and presented using tables, graphs, maps and other methods of display

↓

What the data shows is described, analysed and explained

↓

A conclusion is written about what has been discovered and the results are commented upon

B Choosing a geographical topic

One topic or several topics need to be carefully chosen according to the instructions in the exam syllabus (at the beginning of Section E of this unit). If you are in a school or college, your tutor can give you guidance about the types of topics which are included in your (H)IGCSE geography syllabus. You will be helped to identify the types of fieldwork that it is possible to undertake in your local area. You should think of an **idea** related to what you have studied. There are several possibilities. Three are listed below.

- A topic in geography which you have greatly enjoyed.

- A short study which you had previously done which you now wish to extend further.
- An issue of great importance to the local people in the area where you live.

> **Hint**
> Planning an enquiry.
> The first 4 things to think about:
> 1 Idea
> 2 Title
> 3 Aims
> 4 Data to be collected.

Once you have an idea, the next stage is to ask your tutor whether or not it is a good idea. If it is a good idea, decide upon and agree a **title** with your tutor. Next, you need to write down what you want to find out. These are the **aims** of the work. Begin to think about what **data** you need to collect and where and when you will be able to collect it.

Your title should describe what you are trying to find out in your coursework and fieldwork. Some examples of coursework topics and titles are given below for two topic areas used by many students in their geographical enquiries. Note that many of the titles are written out as questions. Instead of using general titles such as 'A stream study', or 'A study of an out-of-town shopping centre', it is much better if you make your title as precise as possible. For example, a better title for the stream study might be 'How do the channel features of the stream change downstream?' A different title for a shopping centre study could be 'What are the distinctive features of an out-of-town shopping centre?' Both titles make clearer the type of enquiry work that you need to carry out.

Once you have collected the data and begin the write-up, a good title makes it easier to organise the written part and to comment more, especially if you have a **question** in the title that can be answered. A question is introduced by one or more of the following – Where? When? Why? How? and What? Some of the titles are written down as **hypotheses**. The title usually expresses a relationship between two or more geographical features. In testing a hypothesis you need to produce evidence to support, or to dismiss or to amend the relationship suggested. The purpose is not just to prove whether or not it is all correct or all wrong. During and at the end of your writing up you can comment upon the extent to which the hypothesis has been proven or not.

> **Hint**
> A hypothesis is an idea which can be tested.

Some examples of coursework topics and titles

Settlement

Questions

- What is the sphere of influence of settlement A?
- Why is the sphere of influence of settlement B larger than that of settlement C?
- What are the main functions of settlement D?
- In what ways and why are the functions of settlement E different from those of settlement F?
- What are the main features of the Central Business District (CBD) of settlement G?
- What are the differences between two shopping centres in settlement H?
- What shops and services are present in the new out-of-town shopping centre near settlement I?

- What would be the best location for a new hypermarket / shopping centre?
- In what ways and why are housing areas A and B similar / different?
- What are the urban problems of the centre of settlement J?
- How may the urban problems of settlement K be reduced or solved?
- Where and for what reasons has settlement L extended into the rural areas around it?

Hypotheses to investigate

- The number and variety of shops decrease with increasing distance from the city centre.
- Land uses change from commercial to residential with increased distance from the city centre.
- The larger the shopping centre, the larger its sphere of influence.
- The environmental quality of the housing areas increases / decreases with increasing distance from the city centre.

Streams

Questions

Hint
A stream is a smaller part of a river system.

- What are the main features of stream A?
- How does stream B change from source to mouth?
- In what ways and why do the channel features of stream C change as you travel from source to mouth?
- What are the differences in channel features above and below point D?
- How are the channel features of stream E different between winter and summer / between the wet and dry seasons?
- Are there differences in river load above and below point F?
- What are the causes and consequences of river flooding by stream G?

Hypotheses to investigate

- The river channel will become wider and deeper downstream.
- There will be an increase in stream discharge and velocity between two sites A and B.
- The larger the discharge, the greater the velocity of a stream.
- Boulders on the bed of the stream will increase in size towards the river's source.

Opportunities for fieldwork

One of the good features of studying geography is that you have plenty of choice for fieldwork. You do not have to live in a city or near to a river to have opportunities for fieldwork. If you live along the coast, or if the nearest beach is not far away, there are also many opportunities.

For example, you can meet the needs of the **natural environment** part of the syllabus by studying coastal landforms, such as cliffs and beaches, or by looking at the similarities and differences of the physical features between two different stretches of coastline.

You can meet the needs of the **economic** part of the syllabus by looking at the tourist facilities and the reasons for the growth of tourism along one part of the coastline; or you can investigate why one stretch of coastline is more popular with tourists than another.

> **Hint**
> Looking at the similarities and differences between two farms or factories will increase the opportunities for comment in writing up the results.

Similarly, there may be farming areas or factories close to where you live. One type of fieldwork is to undertake a **land use study** on a farm, although this is much easier to do if you know the farmer. Try and include at least two farms or factories in your study so that you can compare them. An alternative enquiry is to investigate an area with factories and the reasons for their location and growth.

ACTIVITY 1

> **Hint**
> This activity is for those offering coursework. Miss out this activity if you are doing the alternative to the coursework option.

Answers are on page 96

1 Make a list of the topic areas in geography which you have studied and have enjoyed.

2 Describe the main features of

a the place where you live

b areas near to where you live that are easy to visit.

3 Draw and fill in a table like the one below. If you have more than one good idea, repeat the work for each one.

Table 2 Planning a geographical enquiry

A	My idea for a topic for doing geographical fieldwork. IDEA POSSIBLE TITLE
B	Thinking about putting the idea into practice. STUDY AREA FOR THE FIELDWORK ACCESS How will I get there? Will it be easy?

> **Hint**
> You can either develop an enquiry entirely based on secondary sources, or you can use them to support your own data collected by fieldwork.

For some studies, such as recording channel and flow features of a river or taking weather recordings, accurate **data collection** can only be undertaken if equipment or instruments are available, such as those used at a weather station. If you cannot access these easily, you need to think more about topics for which the data can be gathered by observation or by using questionnaires (see Section C on data collecting).

Some studies can, however, be based upon data that has already been collected by others. While it is essential that you collect some data from your own fieldwork for at least one of the topics you do, for other studies it may be easier to use various written sources of data. Some of the **written sources** from which useful data can be obtained are:

- census returns, for studies of population and settlement
- weather statistics
- stream-flow records
- traffic-flow statistics.

For example, you can compare the data for temperature and precipitation you have collected for a weather station with that of another weather station either close by or in another part of the country. If you are doing river fieldwork, for safety reasons, you will need to take measurements when water levels are low, probably in the dry season; however, the authority which supervises the river may have data collected in the wet season, which can be used to compare with your own results.

If you want to investigate certain topic areas on the syllabus, there may be no local example, so that any thoughts of carrying out fieldwork are impossible. One good example of this is an enquiry into the causes and effects of **natural hazards**, such as a volcanic eruption, a severe storm, a landslide and an earthquake. These only happen in certain parts of the world. To collect data on a natural hazard that has recently occurred, newspaper and magazines may be the best written source. However, it is also likely that details will be posted on web sites on the Internet as well. The Internet is a great source of geographical data and contains so much data that the main challenge for you is to choose what is relevant to your enquiry.

Hint
Do not download page after page of information which you will not be able to use. Be a selective surfer!

If you intend to make a study of differences in levels of development between countries, remember that international organisations, such as the United Nations, publish tables of data from which comparisons between countries can be made. Your task will be to look for reasons to explain differences between them.

C Collecting the data

Hint
Plan the data collection carefully and carry it out accurately.

At the planning stage you need to consider *what data* you can collect. At this stage you also need to consider *where* and *when* it will be collected. However, do not forget that the data collected must match the title and aims of your enquiry. There is no point just collecting any data in the hope that it will be useful. Collecting data can be time consuming, so careful planning is essential so that you gain the greatest reward for your efforts. Remember that without good data, collection opportunities for presentation of data will be limited and there will be little chance of a successful write-up. Data collection is the foundation upon which any good study is based.

As has already been indicated, data collection can be sub-divided into *two* types.

1 Primary data collection by fieldwork. This means that either working alone or as part of a group, you collect information which is *new* by **questioning** people, **observing**, **counting** or **measuring**.

2 Collecting data from written or other sources, for example:

- data published by world organisations such as the United Nations or by national and regional governments
- newspapers, magazines and books
- information from libraries, tourist information and business reports
- weather data and weather satellite information
- anything collected by using web sites and personal computers.

The nature of the topic you have decided to investigate will largely determine which of these will be your main sources of data.

In the rest of this section, let us concentrate on data collection by **fieldwork** – doing it yourself. Fieldwork data collection can be split up into *four* types as described below:

1 **Questionnaires** – asking and interviewing people.
2 **Observation** – noting down, sketching and photographing what you can see.
3 **Counts** – particularly of pedestrians and traffic.
4 **Measurement** – techniques mainly used in physical geography for studying landforms and weather.

1 Questionnaires

Hint
The types of people whom you might ask to answer questionnaires include: pedestrians; shoppers; shopkeepers; farmers; hotel owners; tourists.

These are a very important source of data collection particularly for enquiries in human geography. For example, they are one of the best ways for determining the **sphere of influence** of a place, such as a settlement, shopping centre or tourist attraction. They are also a useful means of finding out **people's opinions**, **interests** or **habits**. When there is a local issue about which people are likely to have different views, such as whether a new shopping centre or recreation facility should be built, or where a new factory should be located, or whether or not a new road or more parking spaces are needed, using a questionnaire is ideal. There are *two* ways of getting the questionnaire filled in:

- deliver the questionnaires and leave them for people to fill in themselves; give the person a time and a date by which the questionnaire needs to be filled in; return later after the date and collect them
- ask people the questions and fill in the questionnaire sheet for them; this means stopping people in public places or visiting them where they live.

If you have arranged a meeting with the manager of a shop or factory, or the quarry owner, or a farmer or planner, you will need to prepare and ask a greater number of questions than if you are stopping and asking many people in the street. This is because what you are really doing is conducting an **interview** rather than using a questionnaire.

Sometimes it can be better to use two different questionnaires. For example, in a survey of a tourist resort, devise one for the tourists and another for the people who rely upon tourists, such as the shopkeepers and hotel owners.

Hint
Do not waste time asking people their sex and age! You can write in personal details such as these when you have finished talking to the person.

Table 3 Stages in the planning of a good questionnaire

Write down some possible questions that you think you need to ask

↓

Check that there is a good match between these questions and the aims of your study

↓

Try out your questions on two or three friends or others to check that
a they understand the questions and
b the questions are going to give the answers needed for your study.
This is called a pilot study and it can be very useful

↓

Change some questions if the pilot study suggests this is needed
Write out the questions taking care with presentation

↓

Think carefully about
a how many people are going to be questioned
b where and when (time of day) the questionnaires will be used.

Successful data collection using questionnaires depends most upon planning the questions. You should try to copy the features of successful questionnaires given below.

Table 4 Some features of successful questionaires

Number of questions
From 4 to 8 questions is usually best:
- sufficient to gather the information needed
- not too many so that people lose interest.

Type of questions
Closed questions with a limited choice of answers are the best.
- keep the questions as short as possible
- one or two longer, more open questions, if used, should be placed at the end
- avoid questions which people are likely to find embarrassing, such as, 'how much money do you earn?'.

Content of the questions
The information to be gathered must be useful for the title and aims of the work.
- Only ask questions which are needed about which information cannot be gained in any other way.

Lay-out of the questionnaire
Use boxes which can be ticked or crossed for each of the answers.
- Leave wide spaces between lines and questions if anything needs to be written in.

ACTIVITY 2

Hint
This activity is for those offering either Coursework or the Alternative to Coursework.

Answers are on page 96.

Table 5 shows an example of a questionnaire.

Table 5 Example of a questionnaire.

The title of the enquiry for which the questionnaire is going to be used is –
'What is the sphere of influence of Anytown's shopping centre?'

Questionnaire

I am undertaking a questionnaire of shoppers as part of my geography course.

Are you willing to help me by answering five short questions?

1 Where do you live?

Districts in the town (list) Places outside the town (list)

If none of these, name of area or place where you live ______

2 How have you travelled here today?

Bus ☐ Car ☐ Walk ☐ Bicycle ☐

Other – please name ______

3 How long did it take you to get here?

Less than 10 minutes ☐ 10–20 minutes ☐
Between 20–30 minutes ☐ More than 30 minutes ☐

If more than 30 minutes, how long? ______

4 How long is it since your last visit here?

Yesterday ☐ The day before ☐
Less than one week ago ☐ 1–2 weeks ago ☐
2–3 weeks ago ☐ 3–4 weeks ago ☐

If more than 4 weeks, please state approximate date of your last visit

______

5 What types of goods do you usually buy when you come to this shopping centre?

Tick all the boxes which apply.

Food and drink ☐ Clothes and shoes ☐ Electrical goods ☐
Jewellery ☐ Furniture ☐ Books ☐

Others – please name ______

I just come to look around and don't buy much ☐

1 Check the questionnaire shown in Table 5 against the features given for a successful questionnaire in Table 4. Do you think that Table 5 is an example of a successful questionnaire? Explain your answer.

2 Can you think of one or more questions that would be useful for this enquiry? Practise writing them out and check with friends that they will work.

3 Explain why it is better to ask the following questions in a questionnaire.

a Where have you travelled from? (Instead of 'How far have you travelled?')

b When did you last visit here? (Instead of 'Do you come here often?')

Taking a sample

> **Hint**
> You have not the time and the energy to question everyone!

Having written out your questionnaire, your next task is to decide how many people are to be questioned, in which location(s) and when. If your survey is for only a small settlement, it may be possible to question someone in every house, but in most geographical studies questioning everybody in the study is impossible. When you are only able to ask a small number out of the total population, this is known as taking a **sample**. The total size of your sample will depend upon factors such as the number of questions on the questionnaire – which in turn affects how long it is going to take you to ask the questions, how much time you have for asking people and how many people there are who can usefully be questioned. Choose convenient sample sizes, for example 25, 50 or 100, to make it easier to quote results as percentages.

> **Hint**
> Make your sample size as large as is possible. The larger the sample, the more reliable the results.

Different types of sampling

There are several different types of sampling, two of which are useful for questionnaires.

1 *Random sampling* – sampling by 'chance'. This is an unbiased sample in which everyone has an equal chance of being selected. Random numbers may be produced by a computer, or obtained from a book of statistics, or you can even make your own by using birthdays or telephone numbers. Examples of random numbers are:

06 02 59 27 07 50 20 75 43 41 96 52
10 44 38 60 25 01 74 82 83 29 13 36

Random numbers can help you with the sequence as to which people in the street you can give out your questionnaire, or the street numbers of the houses or shops to which the questionnaires should be delivered.

2 *Systematic sampling* – sampling by using a regular number. You may deliver the questionnaires to every tenth house or every third shop or stop every fifth person who goes past you after you have finished questioning the previous person. This introduces a chance element to who is selected and reduces bias.

You should make every effort to make the selection of your sample as unbiased as possible but, in practice, you may have less choice because you are always going to come across some people who are unwilling or unable to answer your questions. In that case, all you can do is ask the next person who is willing to answer. When you write up the work, you can make comment upon this as one of the limitations of data collection.

Think carefully when and where you are going to use the questionnaires. Often it is best when there are going to be large numbers of people present. Early morning may not be the best time to interview shoppers; on the other hand in mid-afternoon or early evening it may be too busy. If you are using questionnaires with people when they are at home, your best time may be on an evening or at a weekend. When writing up always try to explain why you chose the location and time, even if you make it clear that you had little choice because that was the only time that you could manage to go there. When making comments about what you found out in the conclusion, you can always suggest why it would probably have led to more reliable results if it had been possible to go at other times of the day or week.

2 Observation

Good geography students are good observers. Because the Earth's surface forms the main area of study in geography, most geographical enquiries should include observation.

- In **human geography**, land uses are observed in both urban and rural areas
  - the main **urban** land uses are houses, factories, shops, offices, open spaces and transport
  - the main **rural** land uses are farmland, bush, grassland, woodland, marsh (swamp) and non-productive land.
- In **physical geography**, the nature, shape and scale of landforms and the pattern of weather, as well as their effects upon people, are observed.

Some observation will be necessary in every enquiry which includes fieldwork, although its relative importance will vary from topic to topic. For example, in the **sphere of influence** survey of shoppers, already referred to on page 59, questionnaires are the most important method of data collection, but observations about the nature and features of the shopping centre being visited are still needed. In the river channel study mentioned later, measurement is the main method of data collection, but some channel and valley features are better described from observations, illustrated perhaps by **labelled photographs** or **field sketches**.

Observation of land uses

Glossary
CBD – central business district of a town or city

In many settlement studies, observation of **land uses** forms the basis of the enquiry. These include the layout of settlements, types of buildings and their appearance, characteristics of the CBD and characteristics of different shopping centres including types of shops, the range of services and overall size. Sometimes a full study is possible because the size of the area under study is sufficiently small. Examples might include the layout of the whole settlement if it is a village or very small town, or the features of the whole CBD of a small town or city, or the study of all the shops and services in a small shopping centre. However, a full study may not be possible because of the size of the area being investigated; in this case a **sample** is all that can be taken, using the techniques explained in the section on questionnaires.

ACTIVITY 3

Answers are on pages 96 and 97.

Photograph A shows the layout of a new out-of-town complex which has been planned to reduce pressure on the CBD of a large settlement.

Look at photograph A and answer the following questions.

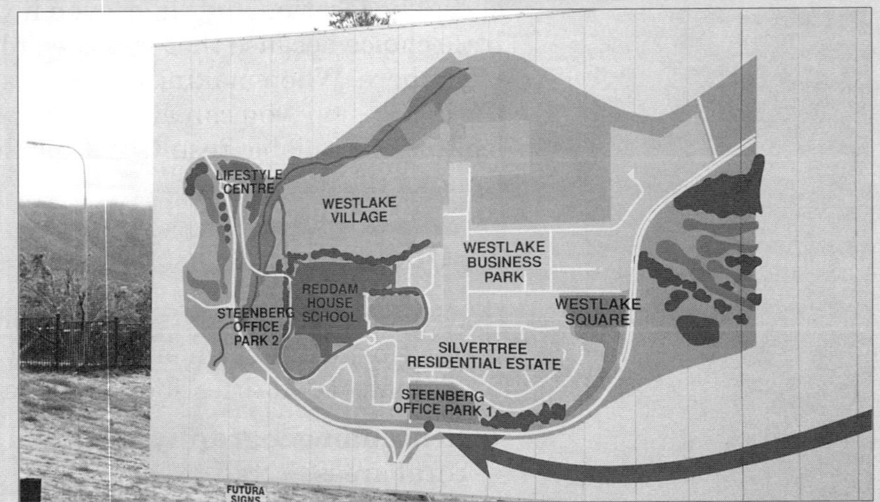

Photograph A

a How does the layout of the new complex suggest that it is a planned settlement?

b i How could you find out how this planned settlement could help reduce pressures on the CBD which is 10 km distant?

ii Describe the methods you would use to carry out such an investigation.

> **Hint**
> A transect line is used to provide a sample of urban features.

A **transect** is often used for studies of urban land uses, especially if the enquiry is focused upon changes from the centre of the settlement to its edges. Doing a **land use transect** means following a line, such as a main road, and writing down the different land uses observed on a recording sheet. The transect line acts as a sample for the kinds of changes likely to be found along other main routes passing through the settlement, which you do not have time to study. How to record land uses along a transect line through an urban area is illustrated in Figure 3.1.

In order to make the observation and recording effective, you need to make a classification of land uses or of different types of shops before you undertake the fieldwork. One example of a land use classification for towns and cities is given in Table 6. Before you try to use the one shown in Table 6 in your own fieldwork, check that the classification includes all the different land uses in your study area. If there are new ones, add them to the classification. Leave out those that are not there. You can use more than one letter; for example, a one-storey detached house would be 1BD. An example of how the land uses can be recorded is shown in Figure 3.1.

Table 6 One classification of urban land uses

Land uses Code number	Code letter
1 Residential	**A** Apartments / flats **B** One-storey houses / bungalows **D** Detached **S** Semi-detached **T** Terraced or link houses joined together in a line
2 Commercial	**B** Banks **G** Garages **M** Markets **O** Offices **S** Shops individual **SM** Shopping malls **W** Warehouses / places for storage of goods
3 Public buildings	**G** Government **S** Schools and colleges **R** Religious **O** Others
4 Entertainment	**A** Arcades **C** Cafes and restaurants **H** Hotels **L** Leisure Centres **T** Theatres / cinemas
5 Industrial	**B** Building and construction **F** Factory **R** Repairing and making goods **O** Others
6 Transport	**A** Airports **B** Bus stations **C** Car parks **D** Docks / ports **R** Railway stations **T** Taxi ranks
7 Open Space	**B** Burial grounds / cemeteries **G** Gardens / vegetable plots **P** Parks **R** Recreation areas **W** Water
8 Unused land	**D** Derelict land and buildings **W** Waste land **V** Vacant land being developed

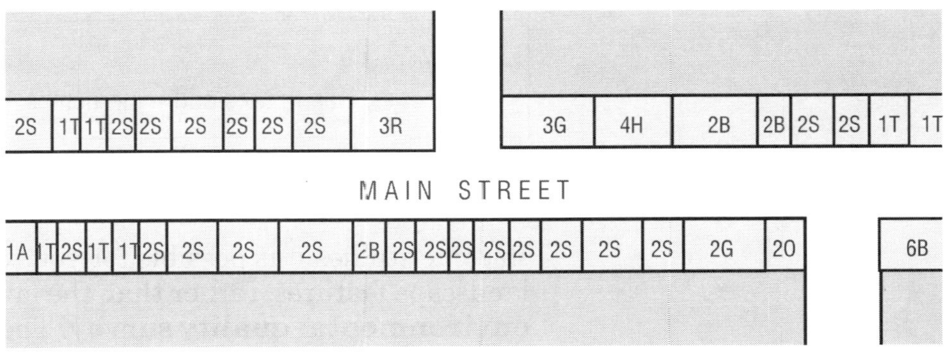

Figure 3.1 Recording land uses in a transect along part of Main Street

The Central Business District – CBD

If you are studying just one area or one urban zone, your survey will need to be more detailed than if you are making a study of the whole urban area. Therefore you will need to use a more detailed classification. One zone, which is often studied separately because of its great importance, is the **city centre** or **CBD.** A more detailed selection of CBD land uses is given in Table 7. Notice that this includes some land uses such as residential (housing) and industrial (factories) which are not often found in most CBDs, but you still need to include them in case you observe them in your fieldwork.

Hint
An urban zone is an area of a town or city where the land uses and functions are similar.

Table 7 A land use classification for use in a CBD.

A Shops / places selling things • Large shops (walk around shops or department stores) or shopping malls • Clothes and shoe shops • Shops selling food and drink • Specialist shops, for example, book shops, jewellers • Market and street stalls
B Catering and entertainment • Cafes, bars, restaurants and hotels • Cinemas, amusements and theatres
C Services • Personal services, for example, hairdressers, laundries, travel agents • Financial services, for example, banks, building societies • Offices and professional services, for example, lawyers, doctors, pharmacies • Public buildings and offices, for example, town hall, government offices, police, library, post office
D Transport • Taxi ranks, bus, coach and railway stations • Car parks
E Places being changed • Empty buildings • Areas being re-built / re-developed
F Residential • Houses and apartments / flats
G Industrial • Factories, warehouses and mine dumps

Environmental quality survey

In some studies it is possible for you to assess the quality of the landscape features, rather than the land uses themselves, using an **environmental quality survey**. These studies are often done for residential areas or for different streets or areas within the CBD. What you need to do to make an environmental quality survey of a housing area is summarised in Table 8.

Table 8 Method for undertaking an environmental quality survey of housing areas

• Visit the different housing areas that you are going to assess. • Decide which features of the housing areas you are going to assess. • Make a Recording Sheet for the features you are going to assess similar to the one shown below.

> **Hint**
> The numbers 1 to 5 represent a scale showing variations low quality = 1 and high quality = 5.

Recording Sheet							
Feature	**Low quality**	**1**	**2**	**3**	**4**	**5**	**High quality**
Housing lay out	Poor, high density						Varied, well spaced
Building materials	Poor quality						Good quality
Gardens	None or badly looked after						Large and well looked after
Open spaces	Absent or small						Present and attractive
Litter and rubbish	Heavily littered						None and clean

- Make as many copies of the Recording Sheet as you are going to need.
- Go and do the fieldwork. Assess each housing area. Record your results.
- Add up the total score for each housing area. The higher the score, the better the environmental quality.

ACTIVITY 4

Answers are on page 97.

Street quality survey in a town centre.

1 How would you assess the following four features of the quality of different streets:
litter; amount of traffic; care of roads and pavements; shop window displays?

2 State at least two other features that would be useful for showing variations in environmental quality between different streets in your nearest town centre.

3 Counts

> **Hint**
> Counts of moving people and objects need to be carefully organised to be effective.

Making counts of objects and people that are not moving is not too much of a problem and you could easily do this on your own. Examples would be:

- counts of cars in car parks
- numbers of people queuing to get into an attraction
- numbers of sunbathers on the beach.

Making counts of object that are moving is more difficult and best results are usually obtained if you can work with another person. Examples would be:

- pedestrians
- moving traffic.

Counting people

Pedestrian counts are mainly used in CBD and shopping centre studies, although they can also form part of tourist and visitor studies. Although it is possible to select the sites where the counts are to be made in a random manner, this is not usually recommended because some of the busiest places may be missed. Much better is to

> **Hint**
> Go and check out the area before you start counting!

> **Hint**
> Isoline maps are explained in Unit 2 on page 38.

> **Glossary**
> ISOLINES – lines on maps which join up places with equal values

do some advance research of the study area to discover where the greatest numbers are likely to be found. Once this has been done, it is then possible to use some kind of systematic sample; for instance, the counts of pedestrians can be made every 100 metres away from the busiest place in the centre of town.

Every person taking part in counting must begin and end at the same time for reliable and useful data collection. Each person needs to be allowed sufficient time to reach the place where the count is to be taken and have a watch which shows the same time as that of all the others. Once the counts have been completed, the numbers should be written down on a map as in Figure 3.2a. The presentation technique most often used to show their geographical pattern is ISOLINES. Another interesting type of isoline is a contour line that joins together places of the same height. You will have learned about these in Unit 1. Figure 3.2b shows equal numbers of pedestrians. You should note that isolines at intervals of 50 are shown so that you can understand the pattern.

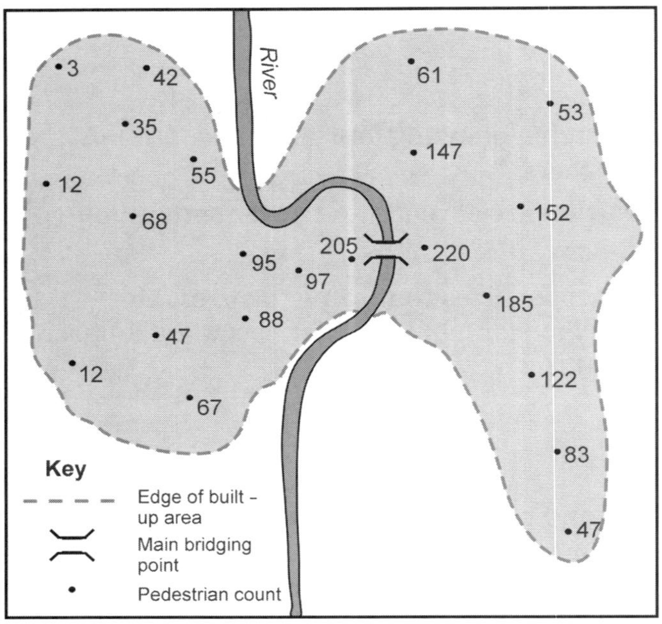

Figure 3.2a Pedestrian counts plotted

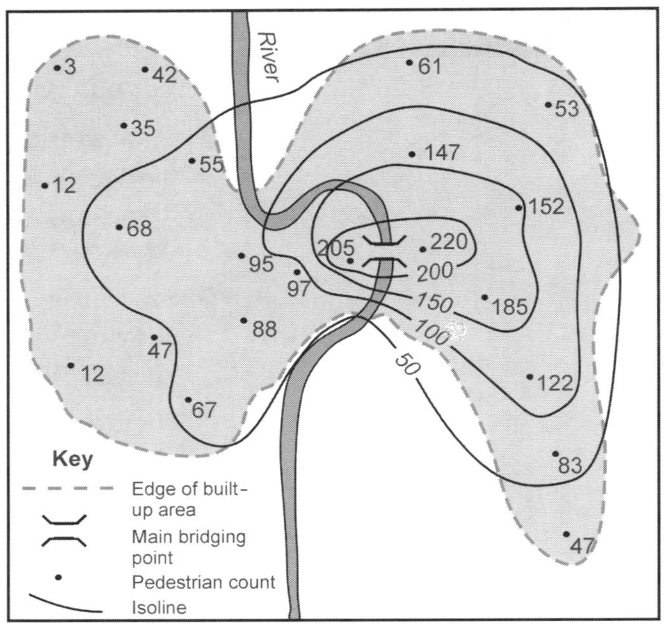

Figure 3.2b Isoline map using the counts

How to draw an isoline map

- On your map write down the numbers counted at each survey point.
- Decide upon a regular interval for the lines. In Figure 3.2b it is 50 people.
- Draw in the lines as in Figure 3.2b so that
  - all lower values are on one side of the line
  - all higher values are on the other side of the line
  - the line passes through places with the same value as itself.
- Write in the value of the line.

> **Hint**
> Think about *what* you are going to count before you start!

Counting traffic

If anything, even more pre-planning is needed for counting traffic. Not only have the sites for the counts to be carefully pre-selected in line with the title and aims of the enquiry, but also you have to decide exactly what is going to be counted – all the traffic, only some types of traffic, different types of traffic, traffic going just in one direction or traffic going in all directions. Table 9 shows one recording sheet that was used for traffic counts. Notice how important information about when and where the traffic count was done is also given. Additional comments were made about traffic flows below. Both are useful when the stage of writing up and commenting is reached.

> **Hint**
> You will have completed the count by hand. When the Municipality wants to count traffic, a cable is connected to an electronic counting device. This device counts automatically as each vehicle crosses the cable.

Table 9 Recording traffic counts

Position of count: Traffic lights on Main Road			Time: 10.00 – 10.20		
Day / date: Monday 3rd. June			Weather: Warm and wet		
Traffic types					
1 Bicycles	2 Motorbikes	3 Cars	4 Vans	5 Trucks	6 Buses and minibuses
I O	I O	I O	I O	I O	I O
/// ////	/// //	~~////~~ ~~////~~	~~////~~ /// ~~////~~ ~~////~~ ~~////~~ /	// ~~////~~	///// /////

I = Traffic going into town O = Traffic going out of town
Comments Road congested going into town
Traffic slow moving

> **Hint**
> What is best depends upon the aims of your enquiry.

The advantage of having different people taking traffic counts in different parts of town at the same time is that you can compare traffic flows and levels of congestion. There are also advantages of taking both traffic and pedestrian counts at different times of the day, or on different days of the week. If your aim is to quantify that one part of a shopping centre or one road is busier than another, taking all the counts at the same time is what matters most. On the other hand, if your aim is to show that the shopping centre is busier on market day or at the weekend, or that some roads are much busier during certain hours, what is more important is that you take counts on different days or at several times during the day so that the results can be compared and checked against your aims.

ACTIVITY 5

Answers are on page 98.

1 Describe how you would organise a group to investigate: How do shopping habits differ in area X?

2 a What kind of traffic survey can be done in the area where you live?

b Make a recording sheet for this traffic survey and suggest how you would present your data.

4 Measurements

Using equipment and instruments to take measurements is most common in enquiries based upon topics in physical geography.

Stream studies

Hint
Find a safe and suitable stream before you begin!

Stream studies are very common because a stream of suitable size can usually be found near where you live. Choose a stream where the water is below knee height when you walk across it. Taking measurements in streams and rivers that are too wide and too deep could be dangerous.

The stream shown in photograph B is large enough to give good results, but it is not too large so that it would be unsafe to take measurements in it.

Photograph B A stream of ideal width and depth for taking measurements

Hint
Using equal intervals takes out some of the 'human' bias!

Next, you need to choose the sites where the measurements will be made. In most stream studies, between four and six sites are best – sufficient to show changes along the stream, but not too many to measure. You might try to choose your sites by one of the methods of sampling described earlier; for example, if the stretch of stream is 500 metres long, you could choose sites at 100 metre intervals along it. However, choosing in this way is not always possible; often it is more important to choose points where access is easy. Whatever method is used, you will need to explain how and why you selected your sites when writing up the work.

For accurate stream measurements, suitable equipment and pre-planning is needed. Table 10 shows a check list of useful equipment.

Table 10 Equipment check list for stream studies

	✓
map of the study area, in plastic folder	☐
recording sheets, note pad, rulers and pencils	☐
tape measure and long rope or chain	☐
RANGING POLES	☐
CLINOMETER	☐
metric rule	☐
floats and / or flow meter	☐
stop watch	☐
rubber boots and waterproof clothing.	☐

Glossary
RANGING POLES – poles used for setting a straight line
CLINOMETER – an instrument that measures the angle of slope

Some of the measurements which can be taken in stream studies are shown in Figure 3.3 and listed in Table 11.

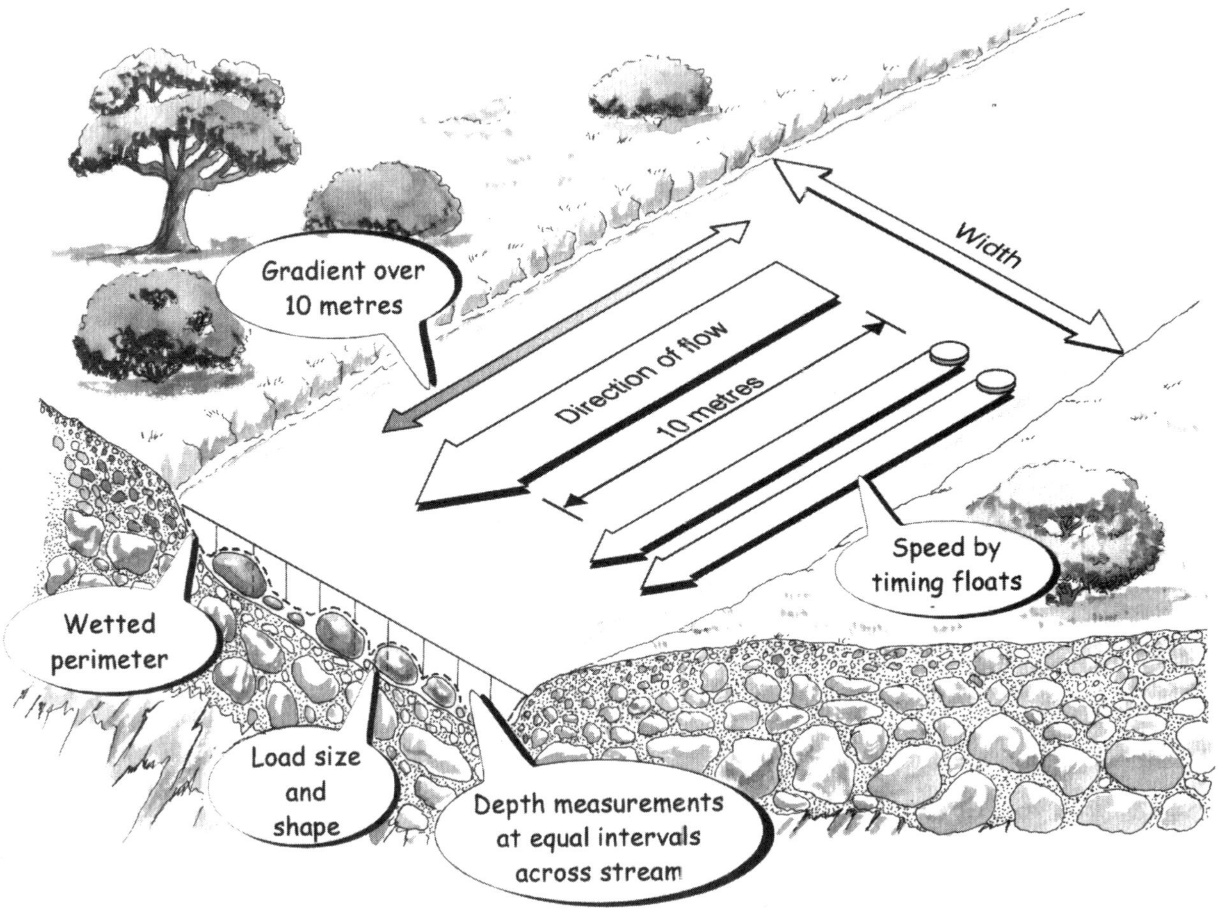

Figure 3.3 Measurements taken in stream studies

Glossary
CHANNEL – the area between the banks where the stream flows
GRADIENT – the slope of the stream or its long profile
BEDLOAD – rocks, stones, pebbles and sand lying in the bottom of the stream

Table 11 Measurements taken in stream studies

Measurements include the following:

- **width of the stream** – stretch the tape measure or rope over the surface of the water from one edge of the CHANNEL to the other.
- **depth of the stream** – mark equal intervals along a rope, for example every half metre
  - stretch the rope across the channel
  - use the metric rule to measure the depth of water at each interval.
- **GRADIENT of the stream bed** – use two ranging poles and a clinometer
  - measure a 10 metre stretch of the stream
  - hold steady two ranging poles on the water surface 10 metres apart
  - use the clinometer to measure the angle between the tops of the two ranging poles B
  - check for accuracy and record your result.
- **speed of flow**

1 with a flow meter
  - hold the meter so that it records speed just below the surface
  - take readings in several different places across the stream
  - calculate and use the average of the different measurements
  - take readings at different depths or in different positions around a meander bend.

2 with floats, such as pieces of wood, an onion or orange
  - measure a 10 metre stretch of the stream
  - let the float go and time how long it takes to cover 10 metres
  - do it several times and in different places to get a more reliable average speed.

- **size of BEDLOAD** – make a random sample of pebbles on the stream bed
  - the pebbles touched by the bottom of the ruler when you measured the depth would be one way of choosing the pebbles
  - find the longest side (axis) of the pebble
  - measure it with a ruler or by using callipers.
- **shape of bedload** – make a random sample of pebbles on the stream bed as described above
  - record shape by using a ruler or a published scale of roundness to classify pebbles in this way (see Figure 3.9 on page 90).

Hint
Read how students did an actual stream study in Section E.

Glossary
WETTED PERIMETER – distance measured on banks and stream floor that the water in the channel is in contact with

One other measurement that can be made is that for the WETTED PERIMETER of the channel. A long piece of chain is laid across the bed of a stream. It needs to go up and down and over the rocks and pebbles on the stream bed, as shown in Figure 3.3. You need to check that it is resting on the bed of the channel for the accuracy of measurement. Measure the total length of the chain. It will be greater than that for the width of the channel on the surface of the water.

Hint
If you do not have a chain then a rope will do. You must check that it is resting on the bed of the channel to get an accurate measurement.

Glossary
VELOCITY – speed at which the stream water flows

Having taken these measurements, you are now able to calculate other characteristics of the stream and its channel.

- Cross-sectional area
  - average depth multiplied by width
  - if the cross-section has been plotted on graph paper keep the same scale for depth and width; it can be calculated even more precisely by adding up the squares.
- Discharge
  - cross-sectional area multiplied by the average speed of flow (VELOCITY)
  - the equation for this is usually written out as:

    $Q = A \times V$

    Q = discharge

    A = cross-sectional area

    V = velocity

Coastal studies

Coastal areas offer possibilities for a number of studies of both physical and human geography. On the physical side it is possible to observe, photograph, sketch or measure features and processes. Because people are attracted to coastal area for leisure purposes, some assessment of their impact on that area makes a useful study.

If you are able to get to a beach, there are a number of physical features that can be observed and a number of processes, associated with waves in different tidal zones (high water to low water) that can be observed and their effects measured.

Depending on the nature of the beach, here are some possible features that you could study:

1 Cliffs and slopes

- observe geological features (rock type, jointing, faults) and relief (slope features, landslips)
- draw field sketches and take photographs to record cliff profiles or coastal slopes above sea shores; sketches and photos are ideal provided that you annotate them to describe essential characteristics, for example, evidence of slumping, steep cliff.

2 Particles

- beaches are made up of different types of particle of different sizes; they may include grains of sand, crushed shells and pebbles of different shapes and sizes, up to large boulders or angular blocks of rock
- you can look at where these different particles have accumulated on the beach and study how they are affected by forces of waves that cause movement of particles

- when you describe and analyse the arrangement of particles on the beach you will be using your skills of observation and measurement
- it is best to select small areas of the beach to make these measurements and observations along a **transect**.

Transects

Figure 3.4 shows different kinds of transect:

- **downshore transects**, **A–B** and **C–D** from the back of the beach, in this case the base of the cliff, to the sea
- **longshore transects**,**P–Q** and **R–S** from one side of the beach to the other, parallel to the sea.

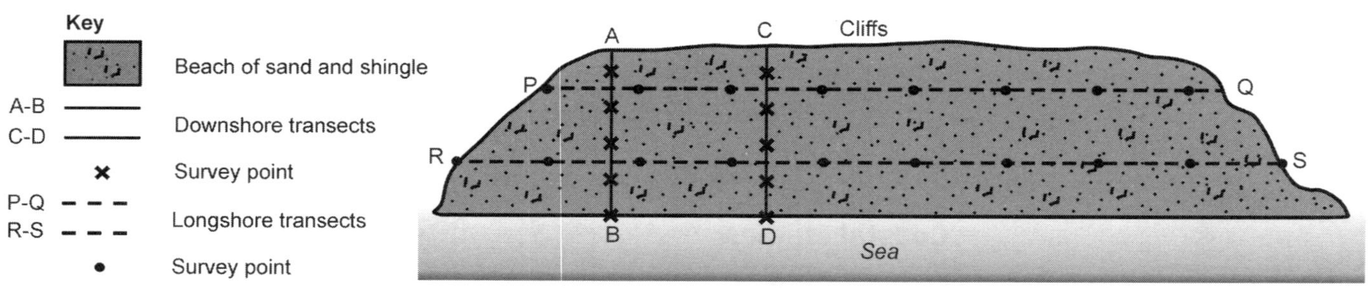

Figure 3.4 Two kinds of transects

Both kinds of transect can be used to get a detailed analysis of what is present and how processes are at work on the beach. For example, the downshore transects, A-B and C-D, could be used to analyse the slope of the beach and the size and arrangement of particles. The longshore transects, P-Q and R-S, are useful when you are studying the movements of beach material in relation to waves moving along a beach. There are two effects of the longshore drift of the waves upon a beach that you could investigate, whether

- deposited particles are graded in size from large to small
- the amount of beach material increases at the end of the bay or where an obstruction to wave movement occurs.

Two kinds of beach survey

There are two different kinds of beach survey that could be carried out along the transect lines:

1 **beach profile** survey

- Choose a transect from the back of the beach (from the base of the cliff) to the sea.
- Decide upon the interval between readings along the transect line. This can be a regular interval, for example, every two metres, using a systematic sample. Or you can select points where there is a significant break of slope down the beach.

- Measure the distance between the points and take clinometer readings to give the angle of the beach slope.
- Measure the angle of slope between each of the chosen points.

2 particle size survey

- Decide upon the interval between samples along the transect line. In most cases an equal interval will be used such as every 2 metres.
- At the sample sites randomly select 5–10 particles. You can increase your chance of randomly selecting particles by placing a QUADRAT over the site selected along the line and using random numbers to decide from where within the quadrat to select the particles to be measured.
- Describe the size and type of particles at the site, for example, measure the long axis and shape of any pebbles, using a ruler and CALLIPERS.

Glossary
QUADRAT – a four-sided square frame, usually made of wire or wood; each side is usually one metre long
CALLIPERS – a measuring instrument made of two short lengths of steel that are hinged together

Photograph C shows a group of students using quadrats as part of a beach survey of pebble sizes.

Photograph C Students using quadrats as part of a beach survey of pebble sizes

It is possible for you to do both kinds of surveys, the beach profile and particle size, at the same time. Table 12 shows one type of **recording sheet** that you could use. The main purpose of the recording sheet is to record measurements but there is space at the top of the sheet for writing in basic details about where and when the recording was done. There is also space for recording observations and comments, for example, descriptions of pebbles.

Hint
More detailed observations can be made in your notebook, where field sketches can be drawn. Taking photographs can also be helpful.

Table 12 Beach survey recording sheet

Beach profile recording sheet

Location __________

Weather __________

Date __________

Time __________

Downshore profile

Site number	Distance from cliff base (metres)	Angle of slope	Particle size (cms) recorded every two metres	Comments
1	2	–1°	47, 42, 35, 30, 21	mixed pebble and sand
2	4	0	25, 10, 11, 15,30	mainly sand
3	6	+2°	52, 57, 61, 45, 69	shingle
4	8	+2°	55, 64, 47, 49, 65	ridge

ACTIVITY 6

Hint
This tests powers of observation and analysis. Refer back to Unit 2 page 44 for help on how to make observations from photographs.

Answers are on pages 98 and 99.

Photograph D shows a beach near to Cape Point, South Africa, that is affected at different times of the year by storm conditions.

Photograph D

Answer the following questions using only the evidence you can see in the photograph.

a If you made a transect along this beach, working from the bottom of the photo towards the skyline, describe the sequence of materials you would observe.

b From your observations, describe the arrangement, size and shape of the materials along the transect.

c Name three depositional features that have formed from these materials.

d State two processes you could investigate that may have contributed to their formation.

e What factors would you take into consideration when choosing the time(s) to do a transect along the beach to record the effects of storms?

Weather studies

> **Hint**
> This type of study will be looked at in greater detail below.

These fall into two types.

- Using a weather station – if you are in a school you could use the school weather station and make a variety of accurate recordings over a period of time.
- Investigating changes in the weather – changes in one or more weather elements, such as temperature, rainfall and wind in different locations can be investigated. You would need to choose locations where significant differences are likely, such as temperature changes from a valley floor up the sides of a hill or from the centre of a big town into the countryside around it.

> **Hint**
> This second type of study is more complicated to set up, takes more time to complete and is only suitable as a group activity.

Data from a weather station

From your studies in Module 2 Unit 6, you may know the methods used at a weather station to record weather. Some are done by measurement with instruments.

Weather element	Instrument(s)
• temperature	maximum and minimum thermometers
• humidity	the wet and dry bulb thermometers
• precipitation	rain gauge
• wind strength	anemometer
• wind direction	wind vane
• atmospheric pressure	barometer
• sunshine	sunshine recorder

Other weather elements, as well as some of those above, are observed.

Weather element	Observation
• wind speed	use the Beaufort scale
• cloud amount	how many oktas (eighths)
• cloud type	cumulus, cirrus, stratus etc.

> **Hint**
> Perfect accuracy is difficult to achieve even at a properly set up school weather station.

Figure 3.5 shows some of these ways of measuring and observing the weather. It also makes some suggestions about what you can do to set up your own weather station if you do not have the proper instruments. The aim is to make the weather readings as accurate as possible. You should comment on the ways of trying to do this when writing up a weather-based enquiry, for example by referring to where the instruments are sited and why. It is vital, however, that you take readings at least once a day at the same time every day. This means that you can make comparisons that are valid between one day's results and those of another day.

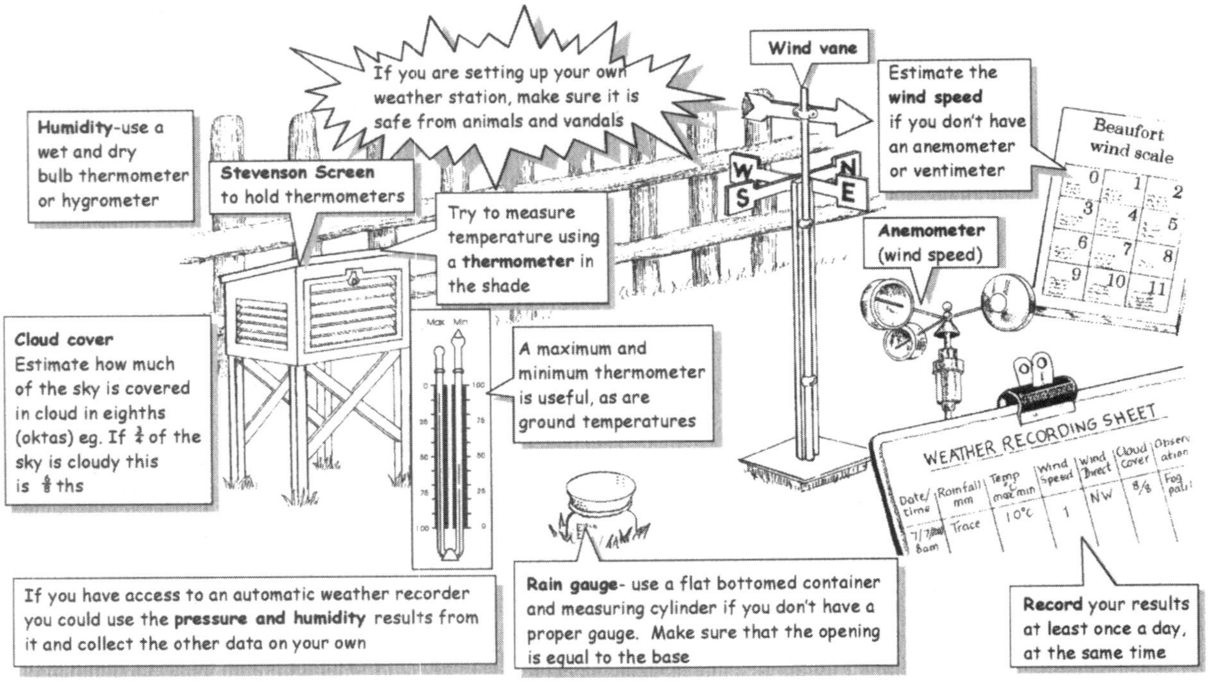

Figure 3.5 Measuring and observing weather in a school weather station

Secondary data

Remember that there are also other sources of weather data from:

- official weather stations
- newspaper maps and forecasts
- radio and TV weather reports.

The data from these other sources is sometimes called **secondary data** because you are using it second hand after it has been collected by someone else. However, it can provide valuable extra information. It has two uses. Firstly, it supplements your own **primary data** – data that you have collected by recording and observation. Secondly, it can be compared with the results of your own data collection.

Representing weather data

Whatever the sources, weather studies provide a lot of data, which needs to be presented and processed before it can be analysed and commented upon. Some weather data can be presented only in graphs and diagrams of one particular type. Some examples follow that show patterns or trends and can also be used for analysing data.

- rainfall – it can only be shown by a vertical bar graph – never lines; the bars are often quite narrow and always shaded in all black
- temperature – it can only be shown by a line graph – never bars
- wind direction – a WIND ROSE is used; the lines are drawn out in eight compass directions (North, North-East, East and so on). These lines, or bars, increase in length with the frequency of winds from that direction.

Glossary – WIND ROSE

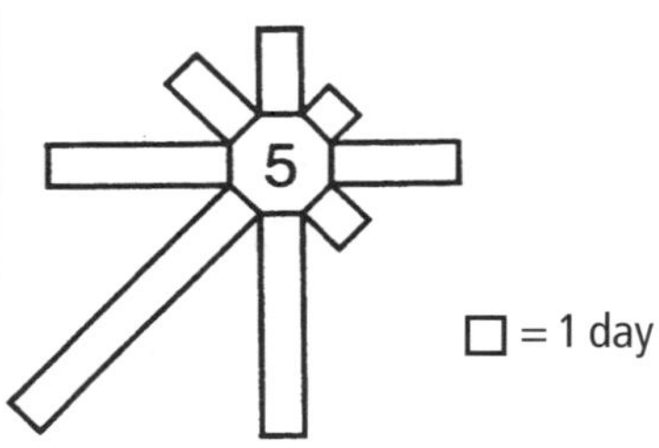

an octagon is drawn in the centre to represent the number of calm days at the weather station

Analysing weather data

Temperature and rainfall values are processed by calculating averages, such as mean daily temperature, mean monthly temperature and mean monthly rainfall. You are more likely to have the opportunity to work out these averages if you are using data supplied by official weather stations. This is because data has been collected over a sufficiently long period of time for the average values to give reliable information about a place's weather.

One useful way of showing variations over many years is the **dispersion diagram**, which is illustrated in Figure 3.6. From this the MEDIAN and QUARTILES can be identified. The dispersion diagram is even more useful if data from two or more weather stations is being compared.

Glossary
MEDIAN – middle value
QUARTILES – the top and bottom 25% of values

How to draw a dispersion diagram

- make a vertical column (bar) for each set of data. There may be one, two, three or more
- choose a scale which covers the full range of values
- mark the scale up the side of each column, keeping it at the same height for each column
- plot each value in the columns with a dot.

ACTIVITY 7

Answers are on page 99.

Analysing dispersion diagrams

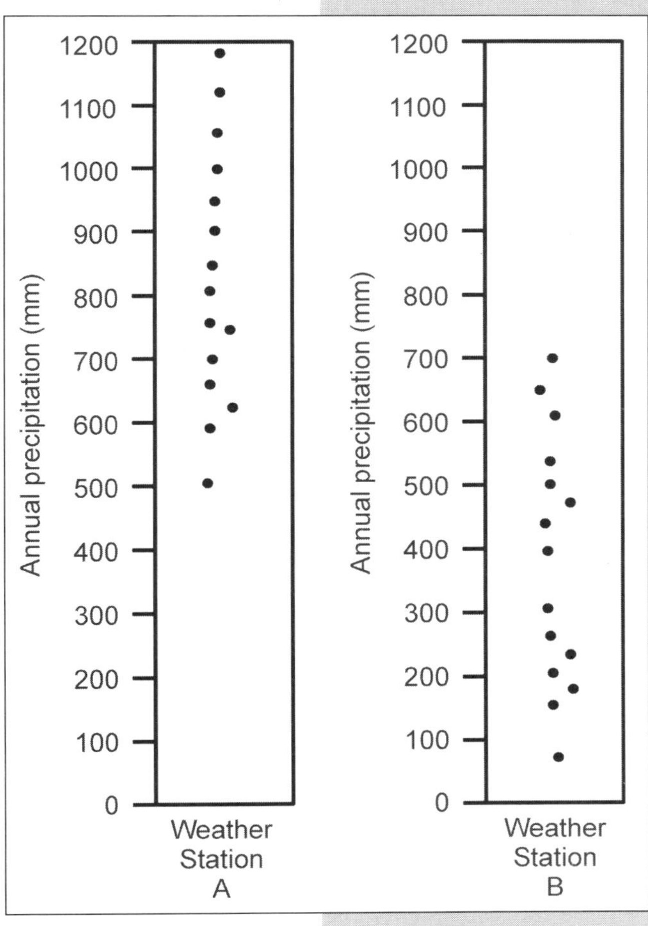

Figure 3.6 shows data from two Weather Stations, A and B. Each dot represents one year. Weather Station A has a median annual rainfall of about 800 mm.
The upper quartile range is 1 000 to 1 180 mm and the lower quartile range is 500 to 660 mm.

Write down the values at Station B for each of the following:

i median annual rainfall
ii the upper quartile range
iii the lower quartile range.

Figure 3.6 Annual totals of precipitation at two Weather Stations over a 15 year period

Completing an enquiry sheet

You are now in a position to finish off your planning for undertaking the enquiry. Make a copy of the planning sheet below in Table 13. Fill it in with your own ideas about what you are going to do.

Table 13 Planning sheet

A The topic Geographical idea Title
B How to put it into practice Location of the study area Equipment needed to carry out the fieldwork
C Planning what needs to be done Aims Methods of Data Collection 1 Questionnaires 2 Observations 3 Counts 4 Measurements 5 Others, for example, secondary sources

D Presenting and processing the data

Hint
You should refer back to Unit 2 of this module which also gives illustrations.

Maps, tables, tally (count) charts, graphs and diagrams are important parts of any geographical enquiry work. They should be an important feature of your finished study.

- **Maps** are an essential part of all geographical studies. They are vital for showing the area in which the enquiry was carried out. They also show how patterns change from one part of the study area to another.
- **Tables** and **tally charts** allow great amounts of collected data to be organised and viewed more easily.
- **Graphs**, **diagrams** and **maps** are visual ways of showing the data collected. They make it easier for you to see what is important.

Writing about what all of these show usually forms the first stage in the writing up of your study.

There are many different methods of presenting geographical data. Those which are used most often are summarised in Table 14.

> **Hint**
> Activity 8 on page 86 describes a pictogram.
> You looked at block diagrams on page 72 of Module 2.

Table 14 Some different methods of presenting geographical data

A	**Methods to show numbers and totals**		
	• bar graph	• circle	• pictogram
B	**Methods to show parts or proportions of a total**		
	• divided bar graph	• pie graph	• pictogram
C	**Methods to show changes with time**		
	• line graph	• bar graph	• time line
D	**Changes and differences along a route or transect**		
	• line graph	• bar graph	• block diagram
E	**Increases and decreases**		
	• bar graph with bars going above and below the zero line		
	• different coloured shading for increases and decreases on a shading (choropleth) map		
F	**Movements or journeys**		
	• flow lines	• desire lines	
G	**Sphere of influence**		
	• desire lines		
H	**Relationships between two values or two sets of data**		
	• scatter graph	• dispersion diagram	
I	**Relationships between three values**		
	• triangular graph	• dispersion diagram	

> **Hint**
> An example of flow lines was shown on page 135, Module 3. Desire lines were shown on page 100, Module 1.

For most enquiries, you can choose the **presentation techniques** from these listed above. However, the list is not totally complete. For example, if you do a stream study, you are likely to use channel cross-sections for showing depth and width measurements of the channel. If you are studying population age-groups for a country or region from a census or other published data, you may want to draw a population pyramid.

Statistical analysis and relationships of data sets

In a few enquiries in which a lot of statistics have been collected, you may need to process the data before you can use it. You can do this by **statistical analysis**.

> **Hint**
> Check back to Section E Unit 2 for examples of finding the mean.

- The first stage is to calculate an **average** or **mean**. This is the total divided by the number of readings. The **median** is the middle point when the data is ranked (placed in order of size).
- The next stage is to calculate the **spread** around the average. Standard deviation gives the spread around the mean. Quartiles (upper and lower) do the same for the median, as shown in Figure 3.6.
- The third stage is to test whether there is a **correlation** between two sets of data. The two sets of data may have been plotted on a scatter graph which will give some indication of the closeness of the relationship and whether it is positive or negative.

Summary advice for presenting data.

- use a variety of techniques
- be neat and accurate
- add keys and labels
- number all of them so that they are easy to refer to
- place them carefully near to the writing to which they refer
- make use of them and refer to them in your writing.

ACTIVITY 8

Answers are on pages 99 and 100.

How to draw a pictogram

- Choose a symbol which looks like what you are trying to show.
- Look at the number of values to be plotted.
- Work out the number to be shown by one symbol, for example, 1 symbol for every 2 vehicles and indicate this in the key.
- Draw each symbol approximately the same size.

1 The following data was collected in a traffic count.

Buses and minibuses 2 Trucks 12 Cars 50 Motorbikes 2

Draw a pictogram of this data using a key.

2 Explain why you should use a variety of techniques when presenting data in a fieldwork project.

E Writing a geographical enquiry and analysing data

To help bring together the guidelines and ideas for geographical enquiry in this unit so far, it will be helpful if we remind ourselves of the requirements of the HIGCSE and IGCSE examination syllabuses.

Those of you who are offering Coursework (Paper 4 in IGCSE and Paper 3 in HIGCSE), must ensure that one assignment is based on the Natural Environment (themes 2.1 and 2.2 in each syllabus). These sections include river processes and associated landforms.

This explains why this topic is not only a popular choice of assignment for Coursework (Paper 4 in IGCSE and Paper 3 in HIGCSE) but why it is important to understand the application of field techniques, in relation to river studies, for the alternative to coursework (Paper 5 in IGCSE and Paper 4 in HIGCSE).

Hint

These requirements may change so check with an up-to-date copy of the syllabus.

Putting ideas into practice – a student assignment

It is helpful, therefore, for us to consider how an actual group assignment, written by an individual student, can help reinforce what you have learned so far. Here is a summary of the actual assignment.

Title of Assignment: To consider how investigations at two sites, A and B, on the River Tuxpan (Mexico) match text-book theories on the work of a river (processes). The contents of the assignment clearly set out the main steps as follows.

Introduction

The introduction justifies the choice of the two sites, A and B, on a permanent river, two kilometres apart. A topographical map is included showing relief, contours and the river's course and channel.

Ideas to be tested

- whether there are differences at the two sites in the flow, speed and efficiency of the stream
- are there differences in the nature and size of the bedload at each site.

Hypotheses to be considered

- that there is a positive correlation between gradient of stream and velocity
- that bedload is larger and more angular towards the source of the stream at Site A
- where the stream's energy is reduced by friction it becomes less efficient.

Methods

These are described for a group study which requires observation and the use of equipment. The students needed to record measurements, produce field sketches and/or photographs in comparing and analysing the work of the stream at each site.

Essentially what the students were trying to find out is:
how the work of the stream will be affected at each site, A and B, by:

- the speed of flow (velocity)
- the area of water in the stream (cross-section) which involves measuring the width and depth of channel
- the gradient (slope) of the stream bed
- the wetted perimeter – those parts of the banks and bed (boulders, pebbles) actually touched by water at each site.

All the work was carried out over two days when weather conditions and water flow conditions were the same. This type of study requires considerable numbers of measurements which you would be required to analyse. At this stage it is interesting to note some of the difficulties encountered by the students and some of the conclusions made.

Hint
True velocity is the rate of flow of the stream below as well as on the surface.

Methods (as described by the student)

A study of Sites A and B on a stream in Mexico

1 To find the velocity of a river at certain points

To do this you need:

a a floating object (a stick was used)
b 2 marking poles 10 m apart along the river bank
c a tape measure
d a stop watch.

Hint
Turn to pages 74 and 75 where photo B and Figure 3.3 will help you understand what the students are trying to measure in this assignment. Table 10 lists the equipment used.

You need 3 people to do this. One person stands about 2 metres behind the first mark with the stick, throws it in the river and shouts "start" when the stick crosses the first mark. The second person stands in the middle of the two marker poles with a stop-watch and starts the watch when the first person shouts. The third person stands about a step behind from the last marker and shouts "end" when the object crosses the 2nd marker or last marker.

You then repeat this process ten times and find the average. First you find the total time taken, then the average time taken and then by dividing distance over time taken you find the average surface velocity. Then you multiply the result by 0.85 to get the true average velocity in m/s.

2 *To measure the width and depth of the river at a point*

To do this you need to use:

a a 1 metre ruler

b a rope longer than the width of the river with a knot every 20 cm.

You then fix both ends of the rope to each side of the river each in right angles to the river flow.

You then measure the depth vertically down using the ruler on every knot on the rope. After this, you record your results and draw a cross-section of the river. Repeat this for both points and compare them. You can then calculate discharge (as cumecs or cubic metres per second)
= cross sectional area x velocity

3 *To find the gradient of a valley floor at a point in the river*

To do this you need a clinometer. For this you need 3 people. One person stands in one point in the river and the other person stands 10 m downstream with the clinometer. He takes three readings towards the person upstream. The third person writes them down and takes the clinometer to the person upstream. He then takes another three readings. You now find the average for all six readings.

4 *To measure the wetted perimeter*

To do this you need to use:

a a 1 metre ruler **b** a rope.

To measure the perimeter touched by water, we started at the point where the surface water touched the left bank and then along the bottom of the stream (over rocks and pebbles) to where the surface water touched the right bank. The readings were in metres.

We needed these readings to help us decide how much of the river's energy is lost to friction by hitting rocks and pebbles, when flowing over the two sites. This will help us to decide how efficient the river is in transporting its load by calculating hydraulic radius = $\frac{\text{cross section area}}{\text{wetted perimeter}}$

The higher this value the more efficient the stream will be in transporting its load.

Results after carrying out the investigation at both sites A and B

1 Velocity

These were presented in detail on graphs and are summarised here from the student's field work records.

Average **surface velocity** over a 10 metre stretch

Site A $\frac{10\text{ m}}{13.86\text{ s}} = 0.72$ m/s Site B $\frac{10\text{ m}}{16.11\text{ s}} = 0.62$ m/s

Hint
Surface velocity is calculated by dividing the distance in metres(m) by time in second(s).

To compensate for loss of speed below the surface due to boulders or pebbles, a factor of −15% was applied to give **true velocity** readings for the flow of the whole stream. This means that we multiply the average surface velocity readings by 0.85.
Site A true velocity = 0.72 x 0.85 = 0.61 m/s
Site B true velocity = 0.62 x 0.85 = 0.53 m/s

Problems encountered that affected the results were described by the students.

"At Site A there were more boulders and rocks and 'white water' turbulence causing interference to the flow of the stick used as a float. These obstructions also caused the stick to float in different directions which also affected the results."

2 Cross-sectional area and discharge

In the actual study, four graphs were shown for each site and readings are plotted. The average of the readings for the group were:

Site A: Cross-sectional Area = 3.72 square metres
Discharge = 3.72 x 0.72
= 2.67 cubic metres per second

Site B: Cross-sectional Area = 3.45 square metres
Discharge = 3.45 x 0.62
= 2.14 cubic metres per second

3 Gradient of stream bed using six clinometer readings (shown in degrees) measured at each site, as described on page 88.

Table 15

Reading	Site A	Site B
1	2.7°	2.0°
2	2.7°	3.0°
3	1.8°	5.0°
4	2.0°	4.0°
5	4.0°	2.0°
6	4.0°	4.0°
Average reading	**2.8°**	**3.3°**

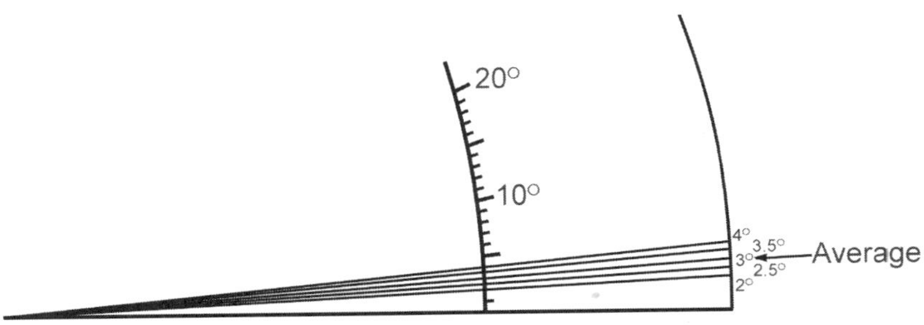

Figure 3.7 Clinometer scale used for readings at Site A

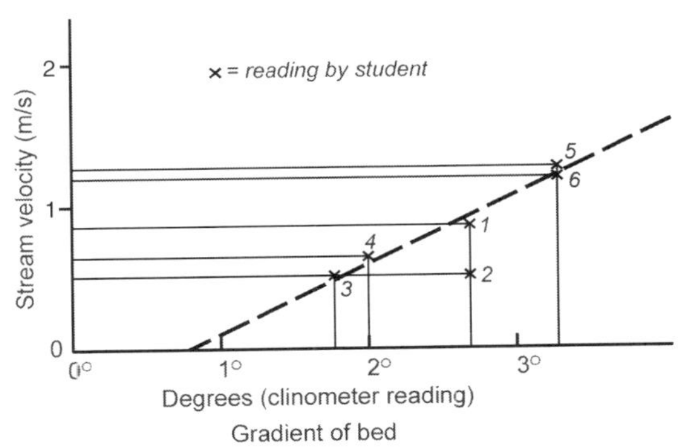

Figure 3.8 Scatter graph for Site A

Hint
Notice that the line of best fit (– –) is drawn with 3 readings on each side of the line and close to the line except for reading 2.

One of the students drew the scatter graph in Figure 3.8 which shows a positive correlation. This means that as the gradient increased the velocity increased.

There was also a positive correlation at Site B but it was less strong than it might have been expected.

> **Hint**
> Refer to pages 75 and 76 for the definitions.

4 Hydraulic radius

The readings for the cross-sectional area were more useful because the perimeter touched by water can be measured to give an index for the hydraulic radius. This was calculated at each site.

At Site A the water was deeper and more turbulent and the cross-sectional area was surprisingly greater than at Site B where we expected a greater area of water. This may have been because it was the dry season and therefore the water was shallower there and the bed was more regular.

The hydraulic radius at each site was:

Site A

$$\frac{6.16 \text{ (cross-sectional area)}}{12.1 \text{ (wetted perimeter)}}$$

index = 0.51

Site B

$$\frac{3.45 \text{ (cross-sectional area)}}{11.4 \text{ (wetted perimeter)}}$$

index = 0.30

5 Investigation of the stream bed at sites A and B

The size of boulders and pebbles and their shape provided evidence of the work of the stream.

It was expected that Site A, in the upper part of the stream, the steepness of the bed would be greater and the bed would be irregular, whereas at Site B, lower down the course, the bed would be less steep and more regular.

In fact, there was not much difference in gradient (as indicated in the readings above) but the bed was steeper and much more regular at Site B. It was interesting therefore to analyse a sample of 50 rocks and pebbles at regular points across each stream bed although these amounted to only a small proportion of the total rocks/pebbles present.

Analysis of sample

The pebbles and rocks are classified according to their shape. They were also measured along their longest axis and recorded according to the following classification, as shown in Figure 3.9.

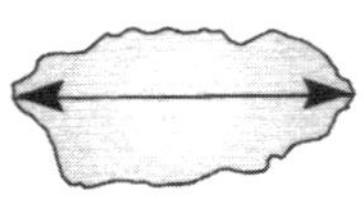

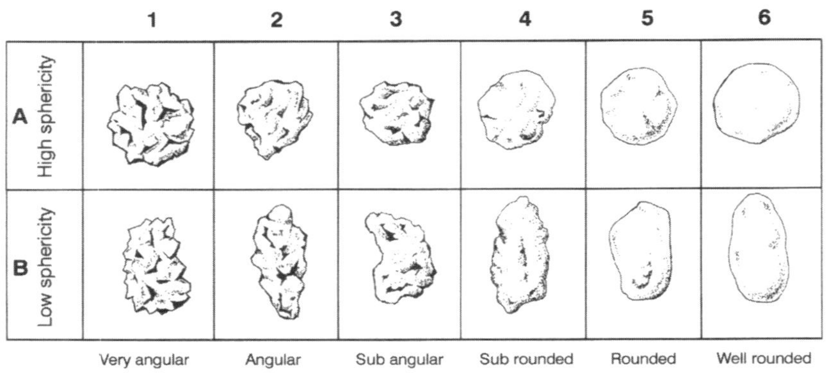

Figure 3.9

Shape of bedload pebbles

Generally the results showed that more angular shaped rocks were present at Site A than at Site B for which more of the bedload was classified as 'rounded'. However, the sample did show that there was a greater proportion of rounded pebbles at A than angular shaped pebbles. This is represented by the pie graphs shown in Figure 3.10.

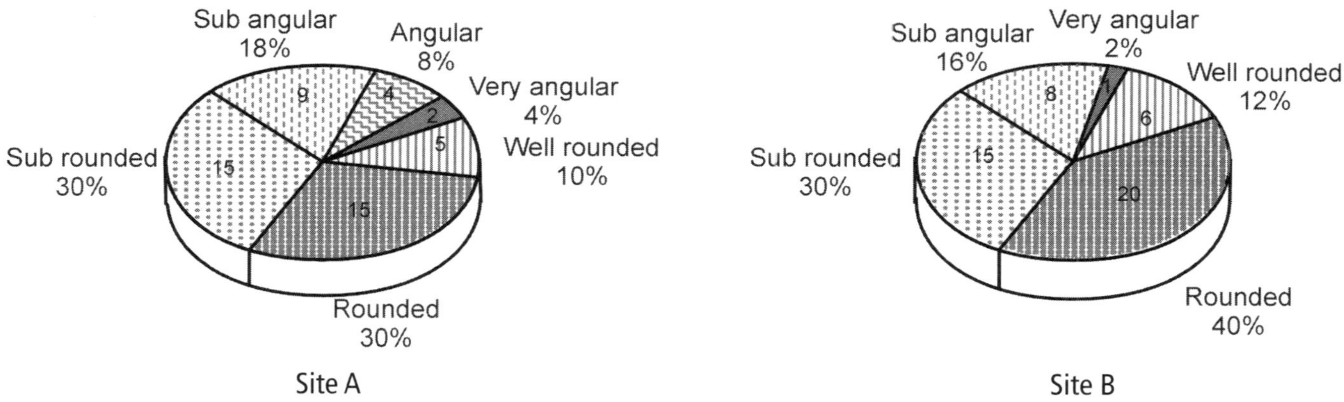

Figure 3.10 Pie graphs to show proportion of rounded and angular pebbles at Site A and Site B

Conclusions

The conclusions were that the measurements of different kinds and the nature of the bedload were generally in line with what the textbooks state, but there were greater similarities at the two sites than might have been expected. This may have been because the investigations were carried out in the dry season. There were also hints that local conditions may have affected the accuracy of the readings, especially at Site A where there was more turbulence and a less regular bed.

Comments on the student's work which acts as an evaluation of the work carried out in the assignment

- At first glance, this seems a complex assignment which could only be attempted by a group of students, although it must be written by an individual student.
- Obviously it needed a lot of guidance from a tutor before it was attempted, regarding sites, equipment to use and methods of investigation.
- It did show how first-hand investigations help students to understand better text book explanations although students (as in this case) should not be afraid to argue that their experiences in full do not always fit exactly explanations in the text book! This may be due partly to insufficient sampling and accuracy of measurement.
- It should also help all students to understand how one part of the syllabus 'River processes' can be investigated even though some students may not be able to do the work at first hand. For example, in arid regions, such as Namibia where streams are not permanent, the flow characteristics cannot always be measured but the river bed particles can be investigated as evidence of processes which operated in the past when the flow was active.

Now that you have read how the assignment was carried out, it will also help you to do a similar exercise when you work through the Check Your Progress at the end of this unit.

Summary

A You should now be able to understand the various steps and skills to be applied in the route to geographical enquiry as described in the syllabus.

B You learned that your choice of topic is crucial. It should be on a scale that enables you to carry out first hand investigations in at least one of your assignments. Otherwise you should do an assignment that considers an issue, using secondary data, provided it focuses on how an issue affects people and their environment.

C You looked at how data collection is possible from various sources, broadly described as primary, first hand data and secondary data. A combination of both kinds of data is acceptable. Observation and recording are important skills to develop.

D You saw how data can be processed using a variety of methods, numerically, graphically or in words. Likewise, it can be presented in many ways using geographical tools, such as maps, diagrams, graphs, tables and photographs, as appropriate.

E We discussed how to write about and process the data collected. This is perhaps the most difficult part because it must lead to some conclusion based on the evidence you have collected in order to test an idea or an hypothesis. If your evidence is inconclusive or your sampling is insufficient do not be afraid to write about these difficulties. It shows you have learned from doing the assignment.

Check your progress

1 A field work study is to take place at ten sites along a river. The aim of the study is to identify similarities and differences in the pattern of surface flow across the river at the ten sites.

At each site the movement of surface water will be timed at five locations spread equally apart across the stream. Figure 3.11 shows the positions for the five locations.

KEY

ABCDE – Locations for recording movement of surface water.

XA and **EY** – each ½ metre

AB, BC, CD, DE – equal distances between **A** and **E**

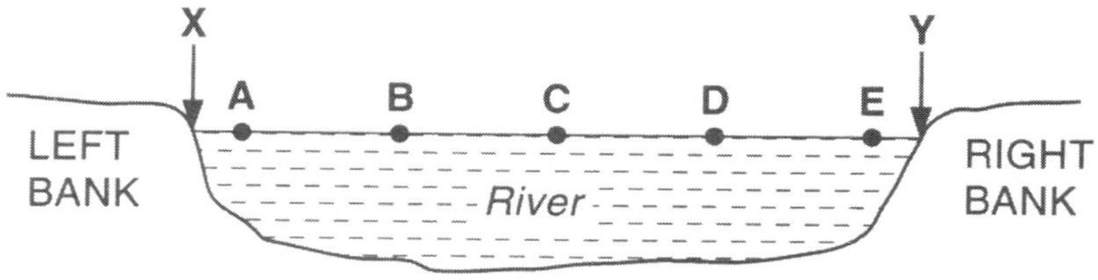

Figure 3.11 The positions for locations of floats across a stream

a **i** To time the movement of the surface water a float will be used. Describe the factors that should be taken into consideration in selecting a suitable object to be used as a float. Name a suitable object. [3]

ii State the equipment that would be required in addition to the float to time the movement of the surface water. [2]

iii Describe how the equipment to which you have referred in **a i** and **a ii** would be used to time the movement of the surface water at each location across the river. [4]

iv Explain why the float should be timed more than once at each location. [2]

v Explain how the speed of surface water at a location on the river would be obtained if the float was timed on all four occasions. [3]

b Table 16 shows the results that were obtained for the ten sites on the river.

Table 16 Speed of surface flow in metres per second

Sites along the river	Locations across river				
	A	B	C	D	E
1	1.0	3.5	4.3	5.2	2.1
2	1.1	3.4	4.9	3.3	1.2
3	1.5	4.1	5.1	4.2	1.4
4	1.9	5.8	4.4	2.9	1.1
5	0.9	2.8	4.4	5.8	1.8
6	2.2	6.4	4.5	2.6	1.2
7	2.3	6.0	4.4	2.4	1.3
8	1.4	3.8	5.4	3.9	1.3
9	1.2	3.1	4.6	6.4	2.4
10	2.1	5.9	3.8	2.7	1.1

Using the information in Table 16, describe **two** ways in which the pattern of the speed of surface flow across the river differs at the ten sites. For *each* of the two patterns you have described, state the numbers of two sites that clearly show the pattern. [6]

2 **a** What is meant by the term 'sphere of influence'? [2]

b You have been asked to take part in a geographical field study to determine the sphere of influence of a town for each of the following services:

1 a local newspaper published in the town

2 a secondary school in the town

3 a large open-air market in the town

4 bus services from the town's bus station.

For each of 1 to 4, state the data you would collect and the method or methods you would use to collect it. [4 x 3]

c Study Figure 3.12 which shows the results of a survey of shoppers visiting shops in the centre of a town.

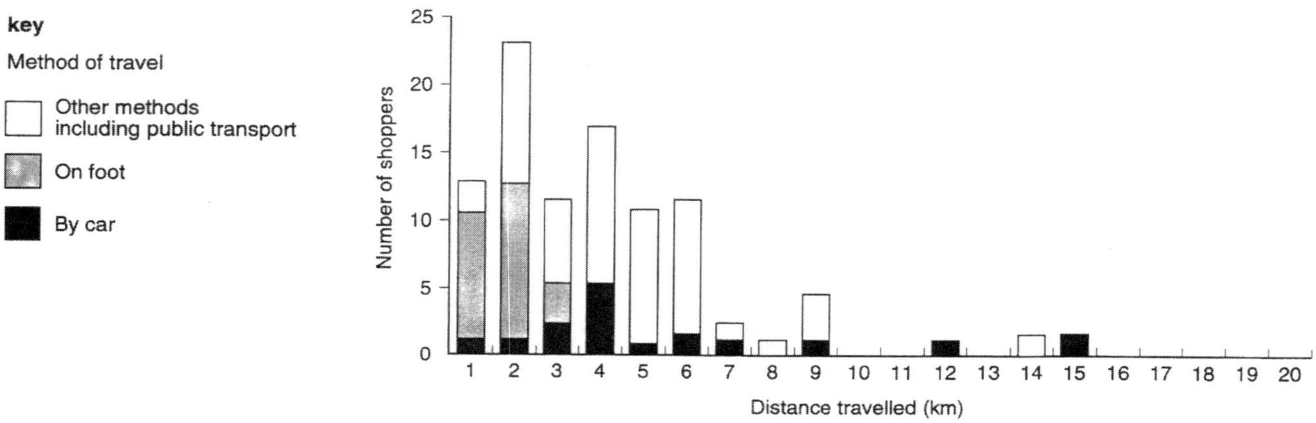

Figure 3.12

i Explain how such a diagram is constructed. [3]

ii Describe **one** other method you could use to show the results of this survey. You may illustrate your answer with a diagram. (An accurate diagram is not required.) [3]

3 Figure 3.13 shows the location of a factory, the settlements where the workers live, bus routes and the cost of travelling from home to factory by bus.

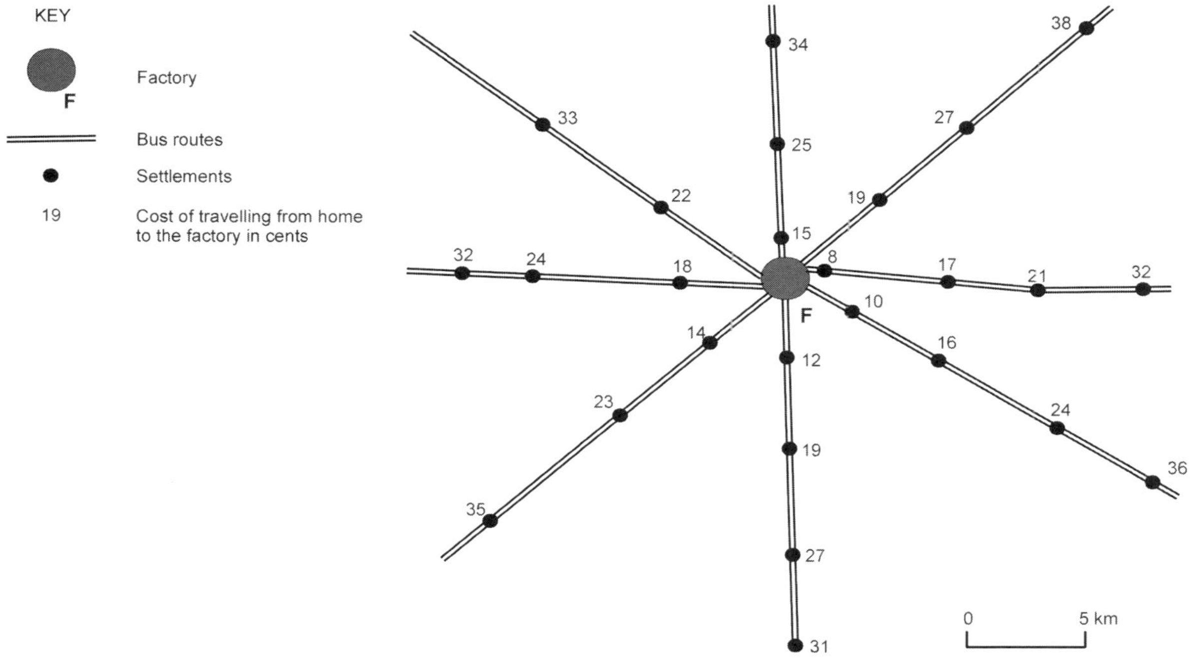

Figure 3.13

a On Figure 3.13, sketch in isolines (lines joining places of equal value) for every 10 cents paid by the workers for the journey from home to the factory. [3]

b If isolines were to be drawn accurately, explain how you would draw the isoline for 20 cents as it crosses different bus routes. [4]

c What are the advantages and limitations of using isoline maps to show geographical data? [4]

Feedback

FEEDBACK 1

Your answers will depend on the topic area you have chosen.

FEEDBACK 2

1 The questionnaire in Table 5 follows the good practice of the features of a successful questionnaire (as shown in Table 4) in the following ways:

- **i** Each of the five parts of the questionnaire in Table 5, contains between 4 and 8 questions that are sufficient to provide the basic information required.
- **ii** Each of the questions points to factual responses and there is little room for vague responses.
- **iii** Answers to questions are easy to analyse because they involve ticks in response to short commands.
- **iv** The layout is clear and easy to follow.
- **v** The questions directly point to the title of the enquiry. The information will enable the sphere of influence of Anytown to be mapped and analysed.

2 Question 5 could be developed so that the frequency of visits to different types of shops could be established. Also details of visits to the settlement to obtain a range of services (rather than types of goods) could be established, for example, clinic, post office, education. Desire lines could be used to show these patterns.

3 **a** 'Where have you travelled from?' establishes a geographical boundary for the numbers of those seeking to obtain a type of goods or service. This will be a clear pointer to the range of the goods or service, being the distance that people are prepared to travel to obtain it.

'How far have you travelled?' This question gives a vague idea rather than a specific location. Time/distance could be more important than distance alone.

b 'When did you last visit here?' Information about the frequency of visits is more helpful than the date of the last visit.

'Do you come here often?' implies a vague yes or no answer which does little to establish a sphere of influence.

FEEDBACK 3

a The layout of the settlement complex is planned to provide different zones (according to function):

where people live – Silvertree Residential Estate
where they can get services – Westlake Village
where their children can go to school – a new school
where they may work – Office Parks and a Business Park
where shops and leisure activities are available – Lifestyle Centres.

All of these are in close proximity of each other and are linked by roads. The settlement is also landscaped (woodland).

b **i** To find out how the planned settlement could help reduce pressures in the CBD in the nearby larger city you would need to investigate:

how many people from the surrounding area go to the CBD at present by road, and the problems they incur (congestion, time taken, parking and crime)

the savings on cost of transport, parking fees and savings on time spent travelling if they used the new complex instead

the cost of rates and rents of offices and shops in the CBD compared to the new complex and also the greater safety in the complex.

ii The methods used would involve:

questionnaires of motorists and workers in the CBD to find out why they would switch to this new complex and to discover what they found attractive about it compared to the CBD.

As regards costs, you could go to the Municipality to obtain secondary information on rates/rents being charged in the CBD and the same from the developers of the new complex.

FEEDBACK 4

1 Generally, for each of the four features, you would need to list criteria to assess from the range of low quality to high quality (1 to 5 index or similar).

You would need to break down criteria for each, probably concentrating on:

Litter:
investigate type of litter
regularity of collection of household and industrial refuse
dumping of litter.

Amount of traffic:
traffic survey by type and frequency at selected sites at selected times

Care of roads and pavements:
state of repair of surfaces
evidence (if any) of maintenance
drains and gutters – clear or blocked

Shop windows and displays
variety and quality: pleasing to the eye or eyesores (visual pollution)

2 Two other features:

On street parking, availability and controls: meters, traffic wardens, security of vehicles from theft or break in – security guards.

Types of shops: availability and usefulness to community – hours of opening and range of goods.

FEEDBACK 5

1 Divide up the work so that one person is responsible for counting the number of people going into a shop or buying from a particular market stall. Depending upon the number of shoppers, one person may be able to count people at several shops or market stalls.

Specify different types of shops/supermarket/market stall, for example, fruit and vegetables, footwear, butcher.

Do the same counts again at a different time and on another day.

Try to explain why you think some shops or stalls are busier than others.

Work in a group and make a questionnaire for shoppers to find out why they prefer to use some shops or market stalls more than others.

2 **a** In many countries most goods are transported by road. Your traffic survey could concentrate on types of goods/materials being transported by road into and/or through a settlement, and effects on congestion. For example, you might choose oil and chemical products, timber, foodstuffs.

i Map routes from different directions into a settlement and routes that bypass or go through a settlement.

ii Select stations (position of count) at appropriate points for traffic counts of the goods specified, using a team of recorders. To get a representative sample select positions both on outskirts of settlement and within the boundaries of the settlement that provide clear views of road (avoid road junctions if too busy).

iii Use different days and times of day for a more complete survey.

b Recording sheet

i Record your counts as in Table 9 on page 73, according to type of vehicle and time of day.

ii List length (size) of vehicle recorded and type, for example, minibus, car.

iii Note any traffic delays, bottlenecks and accidents that affect the flow of traffic.

iv Analyse time / direction of flows by vehicle type.

v Represent by bar chart, graph or flow lines in which thickness of line equals size of traffic flow (thickness of line will be proportional to total number of vehicles).

FEEDBACK 6

a Sand (exposed); seaweed (kelp); small pebbles, larger boulders, blown sand.

b Fine particles of sand on the foreshore;

rounded (spherical) pebbles and boulders above the sand as far as the blown sand hillocks;

larger boulders and pebbles that form an arc to the shore, cutting off the sand.

c Sand beach; pebble and boulder ridge; sand dunes.

d Longshore drift (especially active during storm episodes).

Wind (storm) blown sand forms dunes that are anchored by grasses.

e You would need to consider investigation before and after storms and choose times when the beach was exposed at low tide.

FEEDBACK 7

For weather Station B

i median annual rainfall is 400 mm

ii the upper quartile range is 530–700 mm

iii the lower quartile range is 80–200 mm.

FEEDBACK 8

1 See Figure 3.14

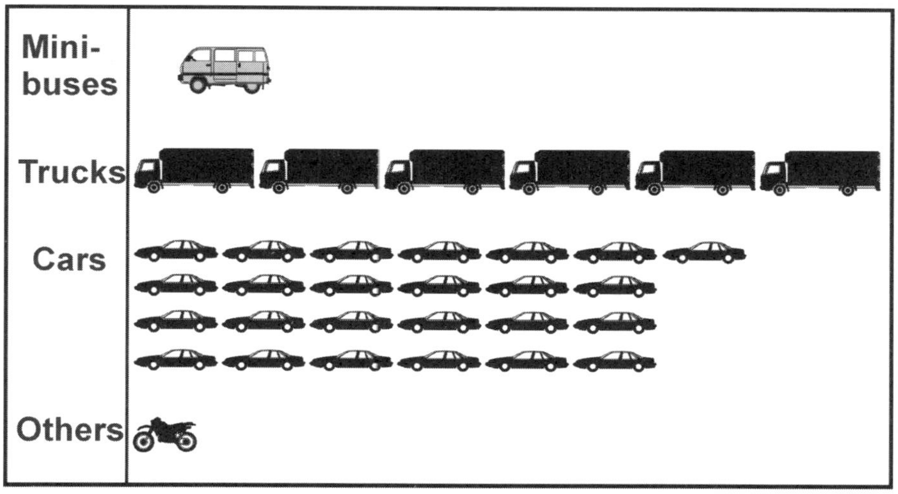

Key: 1 symbol = 2 vehicles for purposes of traffic count

Figure 3.14 Data collected shown by a pictogram

2 You should use a variety of techniques when presenting data in a fieldwork project.

Do not just repeat one technique all the time. **Bar graphs** and **pie graphs** are very useful presentation techniques; they are easy to draw, have many uses and look good. However, you do not gain a mark for every bar graph that you draw, as some students seem to believe. Often there is more than one way in which a set of data can be presented so that you have a choice anyway. For example, for every set of data that can be plotted by a pie graph, it is also possible to use either a **divided bar graph** or a **pictogram**. Which one of these is the best choice for your own study will depend upon what you want the diagram to show.

- If you consider that showing the relative sizes of the different parts is most important, the pie graph may be best.
- If showing the actual numbers is more important, the bar graph is better, because the total is easy to read from the top of the bar and the size of the parts from the scale up the side.

- However, if you consider appearance to be the most important factor of all, the pictogram may be your best choice. Another consideration is that, if you have already used a bar graph or pie graph for some other data, the pictogram may be a good choice because it adds variety.

Unit 4

Preparing for the examination

In this final unit, you will learn how to prepare for the IGCSE and HIGCSE examinations in Geography.

The unit is divided into two sections:

A	The skills which are tested in the HIGCSE and IGCSE examinations
B	Developing your examination techniques

A The skills which are tested in the HIGCSE and IGCSE examinations

The *four* main skills which are tested in the HIGCSE and IGCSE examinations are:

- your knowledge and understanding of topics you have studied
- your ability to analyse information
- your ability to give reasons, express ideas, and come to conclusions
- your ability to do some research.

Papers 1 and **2** of the **HIGCSE** and **IGCSE** examinations contain questions which test the first three of these skills.

Paper 3 in **IGCSE** is a practical paper. Questions here will test the same three skills but will be mainly concerned with the second skill – your ability to analyse information.

Paper 3 of **HIGCSE** and **Paper 4** of **IGCSE** are made up of coursework assignments which are set and marked by teachers in the school. All four skills are tested here but emphasis is given to the fourth skill – how well you investigate the topics.

Paper 4 of **HIGCSE** and **Paper 5** of **IGCSE** are written papers which are alternatives to coursework. They test the same skills as coursework.

In **Papers 1** and **2** of **IGCSE** and **Paper 1** of **HIGCSE** you will be asked to answer any *three* questions out of *six*. In **Paper 2** of **HIGCSE** *four* questions need to be answered out of *seven*.

Another difference between HIGCSE Paper 2 and the other three is that it is divided into *four* sections. Three of the four sections – The Human Environment, The Natural Environment, and Economic and Environmental Issues have *two* questions. You need to select *one* question from each section. The fourth section has only *one* question on the Interpretation of Topographical Maps. This question ***must*** be answered.

> **Hint**
> You should find these questions straightforward if you have revised the topics thoroughly.

All of the questions in the written examination papers in both **IGCSE** and **HIGCSE** will be divided into part questions. Some of these part questions on **Papers 1** and **2** in both the **IGCSE** and **HIGCSE** examination will test your **knowledge** and **understanding** of the topics you have studied in Modules 1, 2 and 3.

Questions may begin by using phrases such as:

- What is meant by ______________________________ ?
- Describe the main types of ______________________________
- Name ______________________________

You have already answered questions with phrases like these when you have worked through the activities, check your progress and end-of-module assignments.

> **Hint**
> As you have worked your way through the four modules you have seen and used many different resources.

All the questions on these papers contain **resources** for you to use. These may be in the form of graphs, maps, diagrams, photographs, tables of data or statistics, drawings and written accounts, such as newspaper extracts. The purpose of including these in questions is to test how well you can extract information from them to use in your answers. Unit 2 of this module has already given you plenty of advice on how to use these resources. This skill is known as **analysis**.

Questions will begin with phrases like:

- Use the information provided to ______________________________
- What does Fig. 1 show about ______________________________?
- With reference to Photograph A suggest ______________________________

Some part questions require you to give **reasons**, or your **ideas** about a situation and come to **conclusions**. These questions are testing your ability to *apply* your knowledge and understanding. After all, one of the main reasons for studying geography is so that you can use the information gained to understand and develop ideas about real situations in the world.

These questions may begin by using phrases such as:

- What do you think should be done ______________________________?
- Why is it difficult to deal with ______________________________?
- Suggest reasons why ______________________________
- Give your views about ______________________________

When you are asked to give your views or ideas about an issue, remember that there may be no single right answer. Everyone has different ideas. The reasons why you have given your views or ideas are the important part of the answer.

> **Hint**
> Do not worry when you see resources in a question related to areas with which you are unfamiliar. They will contain enough information for you to use without you needing to have special knowledge about the areas concerned.

You need to be able to show that you can really apply your knowledge and understanding when dealing with issues and attempting to solve problems. Again, when working through the tasks set in these modules you have had experience at answering this type of question.

Question 1 on **Paper 3** of **IGCSE** and Question 7 on **Paper 2** of **HIGCSE** test your ability to **read** and **interpret** a large-scale topographical map of a tropical area. Which area it happens to be does not matter as the question is only concerned with how well you can read the map provided. When you worked your way through

Unit 1 of this module you had experience of using a large-scale map of Shamva. The techniques of map reading explained in Unit 1 should have provided you with enough confidence to read and interpret a similar map in these examinations.

The rest of **Paper 3** in **IGCSE** tests your practical skills in handling geographical information presented in a variety of forms. You will be required to **analyse** these resources. You must answer **all** of the questions based on these resources. The questions will be similar to those you have worked through in Unit 2 of this module, as well as the end of module assignment.

Paper 3 in **HIGCSE** and **Paper 4** in **IGCSE** are school-based assignments which are completed over a period of time. Unit 3 of this module should help you to develop methods of **research**, including techniques of field work and how to observe, collect and present information for these assignments. These assignments will be set and marked by teachers in your school. When teachers read your assignments they will be looking at the extent of your knowledge and understanding, the way you present and analyse information that you have collected and how you use it to reach conclusions.

Paper 4 in **HIGCSE** and **Paper 5** in **IGCSE** are alternatives to coursework. The questions on these papers relate to enquiries used in field work such as questionnaires, pedestrian and traffic counts. Measurement techniques used in river, beach and weather studies might also be tested. Units 2 and 3 of this module will help you to become familiar with these techniques and how to present and analyse information. The same skills will be tested in these papers as in the coursework assignments. The difference between coursework and the alternative to coursework papers is that in coursework you actually collect information about topics using enquiry and measurement techniques over a period of time. In the alternative to coursework papers you answer questions on these techniques without having collected information yourself.

B Developing your examination techniques

In Section A we outlined the skills tested in the IGCSE and HIGCSE examinations. In this section we will look at a number of ways which may help you to perform to the best of your ability when you take the papers.

Command words and phrases

These tell you what to do in a question. It is vital that you understand their precise meaning so that you respond to the question set. As you read the questions it is a good idea to underline the command words and phrases to remind yourself what you must do when answering. For example, there is a great deal of difference between 'describe' and 'explain'.

At the end of this unit is a glossary, taken from the Notes for Guidance produced with the IGCSE syllabus in Geography, that explains what is meant by the command words and phrases listed.

Hint
Make sure that you study this glossary carefully.

Instructions

Read the instructions on the examination paper thoroughly before you start to answer the questions.

> **Hint**
> The examiner will not give marks for answers beyond the number requested in the instructions stated on the paper.

- On Papers 1 and 2 in IGCSE and Paper 1 on HIGCSE answer **three** questions.
- On Paper 2 of HIGCSE answer **four** questions.
- On Paper 2 of HIGCSE each question answered must be chosen from a **different** section. This means one question is to be selected from each of Sections One, Two, Three and Four.
- There is no point in attempting *more* questions than the number required. If you attempt more you will be giving less detail in your answers because you are giving yourself less time per question.
- On Papers 3 and 5 of IGCSE and Paper 4 of HIGCSE **all** of the questions have to be attempted.

Timing

It is very important that you look at the amount of **time** you have available in the examination. Divide the total time by the number of questions you need to answer and keep to this time for each question. Do not spend too much time on the first question otherwise you have insufficient time for your last question choice. This will inevitably mean that your last answer will be incomplete with the loss of marks as a result.

Sub-marks

> **Hint**
> Make sure that you are guided by these sub-marks when planning how much to write in answering questions.

Another way in which you can make sure that time and effort is well spent in the examination is to look at the **sub-marks** printed at the end of each part of a question. They are given in brackets and tell you the mark which it is possible to achieve for each question. In turn, this should suggest to you how much detail to provide and how long you should spend on a particular part of a question.

- A *low* sub-mark of 1 or 2 marks requires a short answer, possibly a single name or statement.
- A *higher* sub-mark suggests that extended writing is required,

Case studies

When you look through Modules 1, 2 and 3 you will see that special examples have been chosen to illustrate topics. These are called **case studies**. Their purpose is to give you detailed knowledge of well-chosen examples. In Papers 1 and 2 of both IGCSE and HIGCSE, some questions ask you to make reference to an example you have studied to illustrate your answer. In other words, you are expected to be able to produce real detail in your answer based upon studies you have made.

In addition to case studies included in Modules 1, 2 and 3, you may have obtained other illustrations. These may include illustrations from your own area with which you are familiar, such as a new housing development, the development of a new industrial area or the building of a new highway. Other detail may come from coursework studies you have made or from an article you have read in a newspaper or magazine or seen on TV, video or the Internet. However you obtain this information, it is important that you are able to quote some details in the examination to illustrate your answers.

Responses

Vary the type and length of response or answer you give to a question. When questions require descriptions or explanations and the sub-mark suggests that some detail is required, avoid giving lists or note-form answers. These often do not provide enough detail.

Finally, remember that some questions may be answered in a variety of ways, especially when they ask you for your ideas. It is the quality of reasons you give to support your ideas that will determine how successfully you answer this type of question.

Glossary of terms

It is hoped that this glossary of terms used in the Geography Papers (and which is relevant only to Geography) will prove helpful to you as a guide, in other words, it is neither exhaustive nor definitive. The glossary has been deliberately kept brief with respect to the descriptions of their meanings. You should appreciate that the meaning of a term must depend in part on its context.

Note: Illustrative technique as quoted in this glossary includes such things as maps, diagrams, sketches, graphs, etc.

Annotate Add labels or notes or short comments to meet specific requirements usually on an illustrative technique.

Calculate Is used when a numerical answer is required. In general, working should be shown, especially where two or more steps are involved.

Compare Set out the factual details to show how far things either agree/disagree or are alike/unalike. For a comparison, two elements or themes are required. You will be required to identify similarities and differences, in written statements or as shown by illustrative techniques.

Complete To add the remaining detail or details required to a written statement or an illustrative technique.

Contrast Identify differences.

Define or *State the meaning of* or *What is meant by* To describe accurately, giving the meaning of, or the definition of.

Describe Set out the factual details. To give a written account to meet a specific requirement e.g., to give an account of something in terms of size, shape, height etc. May also be seen as *Give an account of*.
Is often coupled with other command words such as *Name and describe* [name the feature and set out the factual details of], *Describe and explain* [set out the factual details and give reasons for], *Describe how, when* or *where* [directives toward a particular aspect for which a written account is required].

Devise or *Plan* Presentation of a particular feature such as a form or questionnaire to meet a specific requirement or requirements.

Draw Make a sketch of. Often coupled with *a labelled diagram* [draw a diagram/illustration with labels to identify its features].

Explain or *Account for* Give reasons for a particular feature.

Factor Characteristics bringing about a certain result.

Feature A characteristic of.

Giving your views Say what you think about.

How In what way? To what extent? By what means/method? May be coupled with *Show how* [prove how, demonstrate how].

Identify Select, recognise a specific feature or features on an illustrative technique or in a written element.

Illustrating your answer Account for by using specific examples or diagrams. Often coupled with *by a labelled diagram* [use of an illustrative technique relating to a specific aspect or aspects in a question to include relevant words or terms to identify particular features].

Insert or *Label* Placing specific names or details to an illustrative technique in response to a particular requirement.

List Identify and name a number of features to meet a particular purpose. Where a given number of features is specified this should not be exceeded.

Locate Find the place of.

Mark Indicate or show on an illustrative technique a particular feature or features.

Match Identify two or more statements or illustrative techniques in which there is an element of similarity or inter-relationship.

Measure Implies that the quantity concerned can be directly obtained from a suitable measuring instrument.

Name To state or specify or identify. To give the word or words by which a specific feature is known or to give examples which illustrate a particular feature.

Pattern A particular arrangement or distribution of items, e.g. settlements. You may be asked to *Suggest a pattern* or *Identify a pattern (or trend)* [recognise a particular sequence or a number of sequences from an illustrative technique or from a written statement].

Reasons Explain, justify, give the causes of.

Refer to or *With reference to* Write an answer which uses some of the ideas provided in an illustrative technique or other additional material such as a case study.

State Set down in brief detail. To refer to an aspect of a particular feature by a short statement or by words or by a single word.

Study Examine closely, pay special attention to, look carefully at and interpret.

Suggest Set down your ideas on or knowledge of. *Propose*, put forward for consideration. Often coupled with *Why* [requires a statement or an explanatory statement referring to a particular feature or features].

Use or *Using the information provided*	Base your answer on the information provided (on the content of an illustrative technique or a written statement).
With the help of information in	Write an answer which uses some of the information provided in the illustrative technique as well as additional material.
What	Used to form a question concerned with selective ideas/details/actions.
What differences are shown between A and B	Use comparative statements to test the changes involved as A changes to B. Factual descriptions of A and B are not required.
Where	At what place? To what place? From what place?
Why	For what cause or reason?

Answers

Check your progress Unit 1

Shamva Map

1 482905 / 482906

2 mine dump / waste dump / spoil heap
quarry / excavation
power line.

3 a Flows to north east / north north east .

b meanders
many tributaries
slow flow / gentle gradient
islands / braiding
rapids
channel width varies.

4 a Mining.

b Ginnery (cotton).

5 a 4682

b Dam on gentle slope fed by streams.
To provide water for cultivation.

6 Steep slopes dissected by many tributary valleys covered by dense bush. This makes road building difficult and therefore this area is remote from other settlements. Cultivation will also be difficult.

Check your progress Unit 2

1 a 9 billion.

b 5 billion.

2 vary / fluctuate from year to year
show a general increase in the numbers of people affected – trend line.

3 1 = United Kingdom
2 = India
3 = Brazil
4 = Japan
5 = The Netherlands.

4 a Floods and strong winds.

b 68 and 52.

5 a 230 m and 260 m.

b 120 and 74.

6

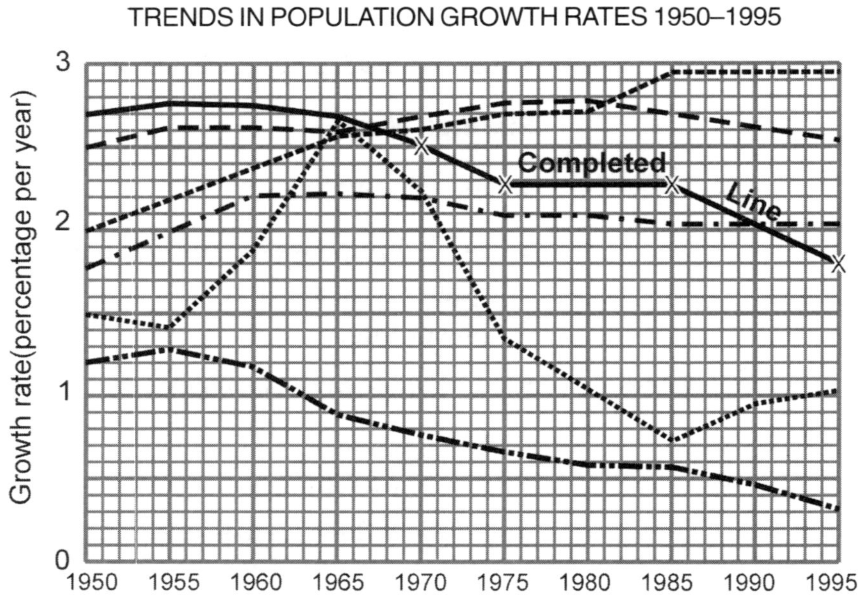

Figure A.1

b 2%.

c 1965.

d rise from 1950 to 1955 (1.2% – 1.3%)
fall to 1980
steeper decline from 1960 to 1965
gentle decline from 1965 to 1980
1980 to 1985 levelled out
continued decline from 1985.

e Decline in growth from 1.5% in 1950 to 1.05 in 1995, i.e. a fall of 0.45%.

7 a South west.

b Spit.

c long (2 km)
narrow
wide sandy beach
curved / hooked
narrow in centre
sand banks / mud flats in estuary
marsh
shallow water
groynes along spit on seaward side to stop longshore drift.

8 a 5.91 million cars.

b 4.42 million cars.

c i **three** of:

North America largest producer in 1964, now Western Europe

Japan now a larger producer than North America

production in North America declined

largest increase in production – in Japan.

ii **three** of:

mostly exported from Western Europe in 1964

mostly exported from Japan in 1990

largest export was to Other Regions in 1964

largest export was to North America in 1990.

9 a i 15 km.

ii 3 km.

b i 2 km.

ii 4 km.

c any **three** of

Most important method of travel from 2 km to 9 km for shoppers.

From 14 km it was the only method of travel used.

Gap in use between 9 km and 14 km.

Furthest distance used – 14 km.

10 a There is a great contrast in consumption of water per person in the developed countries and developing countries shown – 20 cubic metres and below in the developing countries, over 500 cubic metres in the United Kingdom, over 2 000 cubic metres in the United States.

b Problem of scale. To show differences between the developing countries, the columns for the developed countries would have been too large. If the columns for the developed countries had been drawn a reasonable size, then those for the developing countries would not have shown up at all.

c A scale was chosen to show differences between the developing countries and the columns for the developed countries were not drawn to scale but were broken by two lines.

Check your progress Unit 3

1 a i Factors affecting choice of object would be size and weight: The object should float and not sink. If the object was too large or too light (such as a feather), it could be affected by the wind – therefore weather conditions are also a factor in making your choice of object. Suitable objects could be a cork, an orange or a small piece of wood.

ii A stop watch, a measuring tape, poles to be positioned on left and right bank and a rope attached across the channel with markers to show the positions of A, B, C, D and E would be the necessary equipment in addition to the float.

iii Describe the positioning of markers as in a ii above. Then describe the timing of the object used as a float as follows. Ideally three people should work together. One person places the object in the stream and indicates this to the person with the stop watch. A third person indicates the arrival of the float at marker A to E to the person who has the stop watch who then records the timings and works out speed over measured distance in metres per second.

iv The float needs to be timed more than once to ensure that average conditions rather than extreme conditions (for example, a strong wind) are experienced.

v Take all four readings and find the average time. Measure the distance along which the float travelled (measured distance is the same for each try) and divide by the average time of the four readings.

b Table 16 records 10 sites along the river (1 to 10) at which markers A, B, C, D and E are placed across the channel. The table shows at each marker (location) the variation (or pattern) in speed of flow. From these readings you need to make two observations about the pattern. To do this read across the columns and down the columns.

Across the columns you will notice that the speed of flow generally follows the same pattern: It is lowest near the banks at A and E and highest at the more central points of the channel B, C and D. Sites 3 and 8 clearly show this regular pattern.

Down the columns at each of the 10 sites, the speed of flow is less regular between sites 1 to 10 which must indicate greater local variations at each site, such as depth of water, boulders in the stream, slope of bank. Sites 5 and 7 reflect this less regular speed of flow.

2 a A town is linked to the surrounding area (other towns) as a source of supply for different goods, such as shoes, and services, such as a hospital. People who live in these surrounding areas interact with a town to obtain goods and services.

The geographical limits for each good or service represents the urban field of a town, otherwise known as its sphere of influence.

b To contribute to a geographical field study to determine sphere of influence of each of the services located in Town A, you could use both first hand data collected in the field and secondary data to support it.

1 A local newspaper published in the town

Interview the manager to enquire about the catchment of the readers (where they live or buy the newspaper) from distribution points, for example, shops in other towns or villages, at bus stations or railway stations (first hand data). You could question people buying the paper at these points. Within the newspaper analyse the 'local' adverts to determine where the advertisers live, for example, selling a TV set or offering rewards for lost pets (secondary data).

2 A secondary school in the town

The school should have addresses of all students on roll from which you can determine the extent of the school's catchment.

You could obtain data about school buses and to where they travel each day to pick up and drop off students. You could also devise a questionnaire for parents who drop off or collect their children or where they live (distance) and how long it takes (time distance).

3 A large open-air market in the town

During opening times you should interview shoppers and/or leave them with a questionnaire to complete. They should be done on a systematic basis, for example, every fifth person. The data you would collect would require you to obtain information on where they live, what range of goods they come to buy and how often they visit and what transport they need. Desire lines could be drawn from this information.

4 Bus services from the town's bus station

You could obtain secondary information on bus timetables and geographical field of service (how far and frequently they travel) before investigating different bus routes. You could select a total sample if passenger numbers were not too big or an ordered sample, every other person) based on bus journeys at different times of day from the bus station along, say, different roads, both in the town and away from the town (rural areas).

For each sample, you could interview or complete questionnaires when they arrive or leave the bus station, concerning their journey, purpose of journey and time taken.

c i To construct compound bar graphs as shown in Figure 3.12, you would need to complete a bar graph for each set of shoppers who visit shops in the town centre by different means, depending on distance travelled to the centre.

The total number of shoppers represents the height of the bar which is then divided proportionately to represent the number who travel by car, on foot and by other means of transport.

ii You could draw a line graph using the same axes – number of shoppers on vertical axis and distance travelled (km) on the horizontal axis.

You could then plot three lines (different symbols) for shoppers who travel by each of these three methods according to the numbers of shoppers.

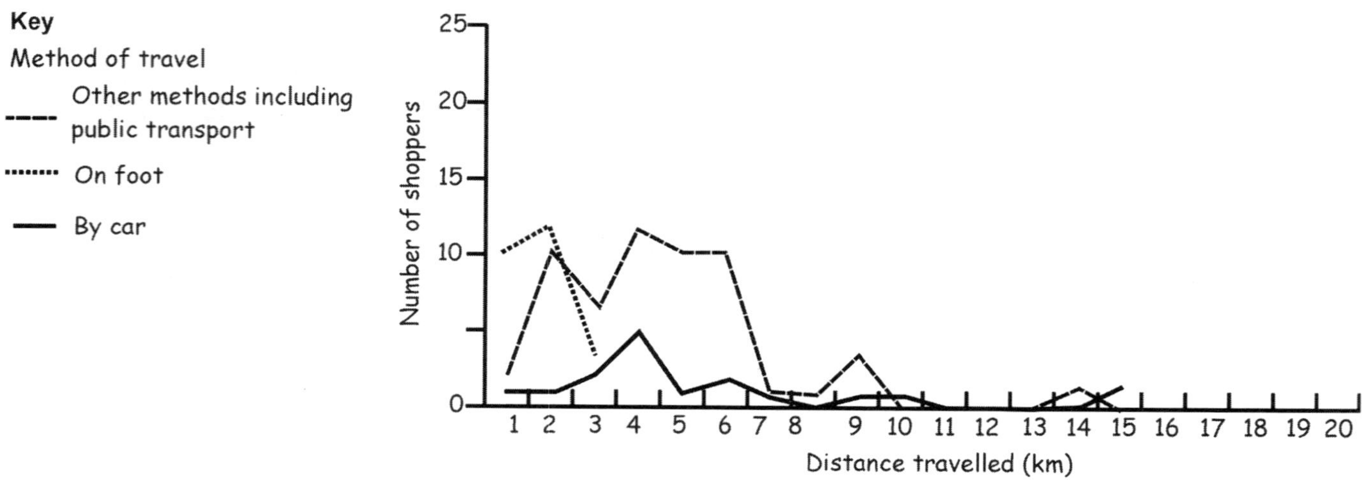

Figure A.2

3 a i See Figure A.3.

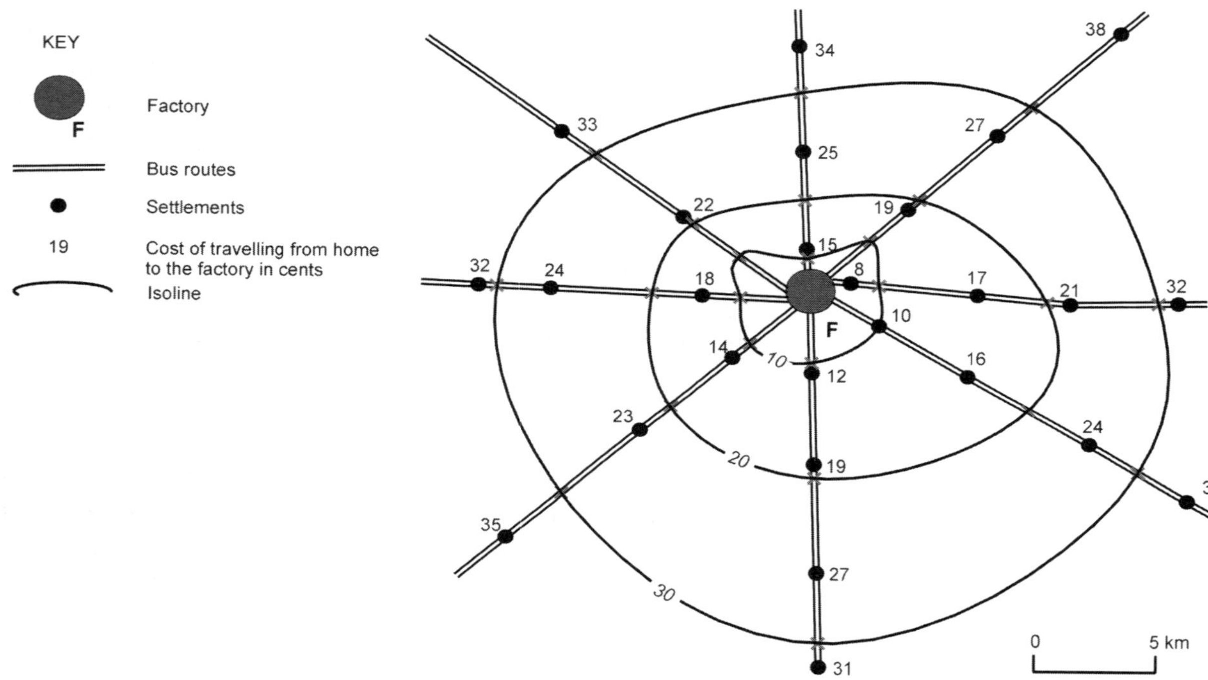

Figure A.3

b The 20 cent isoline must be drawn between the 17 and 21 cent values on one bus route and the 16 to 24 cent values on another bus route. You should measure accurately the distance (=2 cm) between 17 and 21 which means that 2 cm divided by 4 = 1/2 cm would be the distance from the 21 cent point going towards 17.

On the other bus route the 20 cent line would be exactly halfway between 16 and 24 cents (1.5 cm from each). Then you join up the three calculated points.

c Isoline maps show lines which join places of equal value to show geographical data.

The isolines therefore show patterns on maps, such as surface temperature (isotherm), atmospheric pressure (isobars) and heights (contour).

Where a lot of data is available, isolines can reduce this data to various intervals, for example, isotherm (temperature) maps at 5 °C intervals. This makes it easier to read and interpret the data.

However, only by showing selected values a lot of actual values between the 5 °C interval are not plotted and therefore isoline maps do not show the complete picture.

Index

(Note that page numbers in **bold** refer to figures)